A BROKE TEACHER'S
GUIDE to
SUCCESS

HOW TO BUILD YOUR DREAMS
ON TEACHER PAY

Dawn Casey-Rowe

A Broke Teacher's Guide to Success

Cover and interior design by Liz LaFrance

Editor: Nate Granzow

Author photograph by Alison Casey

Library of Congress Control Number: 2019905379

ISBN: 978-0-9906737-3-6 (E-books)

978-0-9906737-2-9 (Print)

CONTENTS

This book is for every person who went into teaching
to make the world a better place.

The world cannot make a single turn on its axis without you.

And to my parents, Rachel & Tom,
who taught many of these financial lessons.

INTRODUCTION:
Why Teachers Are Broke

"You deserve the life you tolerate."
—Steve Cohen

"Broke" is a teacher curse. I was broke. You may be too.

I knew the right things to do but never did them. I juggled bills. I wore clothes coming *back* in style. Some of my high school students had better cars than me. I paid for school supplies with my paycheck and charged my groceries. My finances were broken. So was I.

Ask yourself these questions: *Am I happy with my current financial situation? Do I have a safety net? Do I have enough money to live the way I want? Am I on track for retirement?*

Many of us aren't even close. The statistics on American finances are shocking. We're not saving enough and we're losing ground. Especially teachers.

I promised to improve my finances, but years passed and I was stuck in the same situation. Worse—I had more debt and less savings. I'd made zero forward momentum.

One day my bank sent a survey.

"How much money do you contribute to your retirement each month?" *Next to nothing.*

"How much are you investing?" *Zero.*

"How much do you have in mutual funds?" *Nada.*

The more questions I answered, the worse it got.

"We are now calculating your retirement readiness score…."

I waited for it to say, *"YOU'RE A DISASTER!"* Instead, this is what it said: "You have zero percent chance of meeting your retirement goals."

Zero percent!

I clicked away, but not soon enough.

The phone rang. "Can we help with your retirement planning?" It was the bank. They knew! I confessed to the advisor like he was my financial priest. *Bless me, Father, for I have sinned.*

"I owe a lot. Student loans, business debt, back taxes," I said.

Say three "Hail Marys" and an "Our Father" and don't give to the second collection. Your financial sins will be forgiven. Go in peace, my child.

"And I'm a teacher."

Silence.

We soon agreed I was in a bad place and wouldn't be funding my Roth IRA anytime soon. He gave the usual "save more money" talk but offered neither a solution nor absolution.

Life continued. I tried to make headway but I didn't get far. I was sinking fast. I was a broke teacher living like a broke teacher among other broke teachers doing the same thing. None of us saw our behavior as questionable because teachers save the world, not ourselves.

And then two things happened.

First, the market crashed. My financial hole became too deep. I was either going to dig myself out or bury myself in debt.

Second, I started working an additional job in tech. My tech coworkers and friends cringed when I told education stories. They didn't laugh like teachers did when I sent pictures of fat cathode ray monitors still in use, labeled with captions that said, "Joke of the day."

"That would've been funny in 1995. Today, that's just sad," said my San Francisco coworker, David.

I started to notice many "teacher behaviors" for what they

were: destructive. Skipping groceries and juggling bills to shop for work? This isn't normal behavior—unless you're a teacher. What seemed like self-sacrifice and generosity were the very things keeping me—and many teachers—down. I was enabling the status quo. I had to change or I'd be broke forever.

"*A Broke Teacher's Guide to Success*" isn't about learning to grocery shop on 30 bucks a week or scraping the bottom of the recycling bin for class supplies, although I've done both.

It's the opposite. It's about sending our inner "broke teacher" packing, and building—or rebuilding—the life we want.

"If you like soup kitchens, quit your job and go start one," said Vinnie, a successful entrepreneur. "Otherwise, grow your wealth and help others along the way. You can be successful and still be a good person."

I didn't understand how to do that. My bank account was bad, but my spirit? Much worse.

I became a teacher to save the world. Instead, I nearly destroyed my family's finances. It was time to get rid of the "broke teacher" in me. This book is that story. It might be your story too.

"Broke Teacher" started as a joke. I was posting "broke jokes" and "recycled food" on Facebook for a teacher who moved to Oklahoma to work for half her Massachusetts pay. I made a website featuring 10-cent recipes, couponing, lifestyle hacks, and articles like "The Best Places in Town to Steal Pens for Your Classroom."

The teacher's situation got worse. I wanted to write about it.

"I wish you would," she said. As I wrote, I realized something. Teacher problems are bigger than Oklahoma. They're national.

I was no better off because the pay in my region was higher—that just meant I spent more on my classroom.

I was broke and broken. It was time to fix both.

I finished this book long before teacher walkouts swept the nation. In fact, it's been done and sitting on a desk for more than two years but I didn't release it. I was too tired of discussing "teacher problems" to talk about these things. I was writing about being valuable, but I didn't feel valuable at all. So I put this manuscript down and listened to other teachers. I discovered I wasn't alone.

Many educators—and Americans in general—are in the same space. Feeling hopeless. "Broke Teacher" isn't a joke. It's a national epidemic.

This book takes aim at two things: declining teacher spirit and educator finances. We'll start fixing both. It's critical. I can't tell kids to be successful while I'm broke—they're too slick for that. I have to improve myself first.

For years, I tried to salvage my finances by being ultra-frugal. I failed. The solution isn't shaking out couch cushions for quarters, it's making more of them.

In the past few years, teachers have made headlines in many states, but effective reform has barely begun. This book isn't about America throwing schools a bone. It's about you—individually—looking in the mirror and seeing your value, then using that value to build your perfect life.

I learned this: I can't change education. I can only change me.

So, that's what I started to do.

I'll be honest, I didn't like the first draft of this book. It was B-grade financial literature written by a person who wasn't wealthy. There are far better people out there to read. Read Dave Ramsey, Suze Orman, Clark Howard, James Altucher, or Ramit Sethi—that's who I give my students. I let that draft decompose and die.

I didn't need to write a financial literacy book. I had to tell a story. The story is about the limiting things teachers do (and believe) every day ("for the kids") without realizing we're sabotaging our well-being and long-term financial health. It has to stop.

My situation was embarrassing to me, my debt a source of terror, but the guilt of saying "no" kept me frozen until one day I had only one choice: buy food or things for the class.

"You're light years ahead of me; you're starting from zero," I told my first financial literacy class.

I couldn't tell upperclassmen how to be successful when I had a pile of debt, so I decided to come clean. "I'm going to tell you how I got my butt kicked so you won't." I built a whole course around my financial mistakes from college to the present day.

We talked about student loans, ROI when choosing a career, business debt, the cost of bad contracts, credit cards, opportunity cost, and taxes. We looked at how to turn passions into cash. I taught "money skills:" the skills I'd started to use to freelance, contract, and make more on the side. "This skill is my gift to you. I use it to make money—outside of here—*for real.*"

"For real." I told them I didn't want to spend the rest of my life waiting for the next paycheck. I wanted to build something more—and so should they.

Suddenly, everyone wanted to learn what I was teaching. It had value. It wasn't from a book. It was from life—lessons that could make them money—lessons that were saving me at the same time.

"Miss, I was at a dinner and I gave a speech like you taught us. Rich people came up to me and handed me checks." It was the girl who hated public speaking the most. She had cried and threatened to vomit when it was her turn, but I made her speak anyway.

I said, "That's OK. We have paper towels. This is important. I make money with this skill." She gave her speech and cursed me.

Now she was the state gymnastics champion delivering a

keynote speech to the foundation that funded her training when her family couldn't pay. She raised almost $40,000 in one night.

But the day Olivia cut up her high-interest Victoria's Secret credit card, I knew I was onto something powerful.

Anyone can fix their finances—from broke teacher to soon-to-be-rich student. It's simple math combined with a mindset change, not rocket science.

Several students in that class said it was one of their most valuable experiences in school.

I tell them this: "It was for me, too."

"Every moment we live with debt, we're stealing from our future," says financial literacy educator Meggan Orenstein. Meggan teaches finances to military families. She helps hundreds of people set and achieve goals.

I see teachers stealing from their futures from day one. They walk into schools waving Visas and Mastercards.

"My students need this," they say.

STOP!

This book attacks the myth that you must fund your classroom to be a good teacher.

"I'm going into teaching because the pay's amazing," said no aspiring teacher ever. It took a personal disaster before I stopped destructive spending and started fixing my finances. I hope you'll let these stories—rather than your credit card bill—change your thinking.

If you've taken a teaching job you can't afford, overspent on your classroom, racked up debt, or fallen in love with education but secretly wish you'd chosen engineering, I hope this helps.

I can't control teacher pay, but I can avoid doing things that keep me down. The next generation of teachers depends on it. What kid wants a career with a lifetime guarantee of struggle and poverty where all the heroes are destitute?

Not one.

I set out to accomplish a few things. First, to answer, "What is it I really want? If I could have *anything*? If money wasn't an object?" I discovered I'd been settling for much less and that much of the list didn't require cash. It required a mindset change.

Next, I asked, "What skills do I have that people will pay me for so I can dig myself out?" Turns out quite a lot. Many of them are standard "teacher skills," so you have them too.

Finally, I learned to recognize and say no to things keeping me from my goals, things like overcommitting and spending my paycheck on my job.

Once I identified the issues, I began to rebuild, taking small steps every day.

It's a journey. A lifelong one. But now, I know this: I don't have to be broke to be a teacher. In fact, I shouldn't be. And it's all within my control.

That's the lesson I learned. The one I hope to share.

TOP REASONS YOU'RE BROKE
...but not for long!

- Your student loans are 50 times more than your salary.

- You give away pencils, pens, notebooks, and snacks every day.

- You pay for your own conferences and professional development.

- Your classroom looks like it was professionally decorated—by you.

- You never say no to a fundraiser.

- You pay for tickets when you chaperone.

- You buy your own work laptop, software, and subscriptions.

- You restock everything in your class.

- You "lend" lunch money or you cook for the school regularly.

- You're out of everything. You buy more, "Just this once."

If this describes you, let's get busy.

SECTION ONE
Are You Broke?

*"You have to go broke three times to learn
how to make a living."*
—Casey Stengel

*"Being broke is a temporary situation.
Being poor is a state of mind."*
—Mike Todd

Objective

Recognize and leave "broke teacher thinking" behind.

Ask and answer:
"If life could be anything, what would I want it to be?"

CHAPTER ONE
How I Discovered I Was Broke

*"The world breaks everyone, and afterward, some are strong
at the broken places."*
—Ernest Hemingway

"Hey," said my bank account, "You've gotta put some money in here!"

I'd been teaching for a while, spending away. One day, I realized I was broke.

If you're a teacher, chances are you don't live large, but going broke doesn't happen overnight. Every time I bought "a little something" for my classroom, savings dwindled until, one day, my checking account staged a revolution.

I was broke.

Ramen noodle broke, and I'd have a long way to go before I could stand on solid ground once more. My checking account was the Oklahoma Dust Bowl.

It wasn't always that way. I worked for an insurance company for almost a decade after college. It paid well enough that I could do what I wanted—within reason. If I went a bit nuts, I'd pay it off with my December bonus and get back on track.

Schools don't pay bonuses. Every once in a while there's a small stipend for a committee or coaching. It's more of a "go buy yourself a coffee" deal, not a real bonus.

One of my friends works in sales. She gets bonuses with four and five zeroes attached. In education, ours have one zero, with no numbers in front. If I got behind, I stayed behind. There was no quarterly windfall to wipe up the mess, no matching 401K, and no stock options.

Every year I ended up more in the hole. My hole got deeper until it looked like a grave.

"Bills are due," my bank account said. "Car, mortgage, student loans...." I was underwater without a life preserver.

How did this happen? I planned ahead when I left Corporate America to teach. I knew the pay would be lower. I consolidated student loans and lived simply. We owned a growing business. Things were good. Every year I made a little more money teaching. It wasn't my previous salary, but it was progress.

Then, the economy crashed.

People panicked, markets tanked, and the Roaring Nineties came to an end. Jobs and businesses disappeared. The age of free and easy credit—of living on the edge, on margin—was over. The piper needed to be paid.

Our business suffered, leaving us with one salary—mine. We owed everyone: banks, commercial landlords, and Uncle Sam. I'd planned for emergencies, not the apocalypse.

Big mistake. The perfect storm is always out there. The difference between sinking, treading water, and getting safely to shore is whether your lifeboat has been prepared well in advance. My lifeboat had a big hole.

I discovered it when I went to pay a bill. We'd replaced our puppy-stained rugs with hardwood floors. "Zero percent interest," said the big print, "for the first six months." I wasn't concerned. Our tax refund would take care of it. The refund never came.

"I used it to pay the mortgage the last two months," my husband said. He said the business was having cash-flow problems. It owed two month's rent to the landlord with the third just days away. He'd stopped taking a salary months earlier, but figured it would be temporary. It wasn't.

Just like that, my best-laid plans were jackhammered apart. My teacher pay couldn't cover the household expenses, the business was in trouble, and the bill for the floors was due.

The first lesson is this: Don't buy on margin. That's straight out of the 1929 playbook. America ignored it during the 1990s when credit flowed like water. "Need a loan? Credit card? New rugs? No problem! Sign on the dotted line."

I knew better. I come from a banking family. My parents were thrifty. Now our second income was gone and my "zero-percent" loan would convert to a 27-percent nightmare in an economy designed by the Four Horsemen of the Apocalypse. Any loan shark would've been proud.

We'd already borrowed against our house to buy the business, then remortgaged to keep it afloat. The house we bought for $87,000 at a HUD auction had a $250,000 note.

If lesson number one is "Don't buy on margin," lesson two is this: Never use credit to pay off debt. That'll kill you faster than blowing off lesson one. We thought we'd been building our future. What we built was a house of cards.

That was when the economy came to a grinding halt. We didn't know it yet, but it was the start of the 2008 mortgage crisis. Banks ducked and covered. They stopped lending. One lender offered to convert our low-interest mortgage to a higher variable-rate note. My credit score was outstanding—a variable note was a big red flag.

"You can convert this to a fixed-rate in three years," he said. "You have $100,000 in equity."

Red flag number two. We had a small raised ranch near the airport; there was no way it could be worth that much.

It was. We were at the top of a housing bubble that was about to pop. If I'd said yes to that offer, I would've sealed myself in a coffin of "equity" created by Wall Street and jumped into a big, fat grave of debt.

"How can I be sure a fixed-rate mortgage will be available in three years?" No one can predict that far out. If I couldn't refinance, the payment would double.

"People do this all the time," the lender said.

Those exact same people lost their homes as payments skyrocketed due to bad mortgages like this one. Banks foreclosed. It was the Wild West. No guarantees. The banks got bailed out—they were "too big to fail." The people? They were left standing on the sidewalk.

"No, thank you," I said.

That "no" was the first good decision I made in a long time. With no rescue loan or second income on the horizon, I'd have to stop the bleeding and recover—all by myself.

I shifted money, stopped spending, scraped together dimes, and asked Peter to pay Paul one last time. The numbers just about lined up if I maintained serious discipline.

Lesson three: Don't plan for one bump in the road. There will be several. There will be bumps, giant potholes, a few brick walls, and a Molotov cocktail.

Just when I thought I could survive, I got *The Letter* in the mail.

The Letter looked like junk mail. I nearly tossed it, which was what the sender intended.

It wasn't junk. It was a notice from my credit card company doubling my interest rates. "If you don't reply in writing, we assume you agree."

"Why would I agree to this?" I called customer service. "I have a perfect credit score." I was making progress reducing debt at eight percent interest but I wouldn't at 15 percent. "There must be some mistake."

No mistake. It was all in the fine print America doesn't read. As the economy crumbled, people started defaulting on their credit cards, too. Credit card companies raised rates for everyone.

Credit card companies can do nearly anything as long as they give notice. "You agree to give your first-born child and three sheep to some guy in Mongolia." You must refuse in writing, or it sticks.

In pre-crash America, I was a creditor's dream. I paid my bills but carried a balance so I paid a ton of interest. Post-crash, I was a risk. I owed everyone. "Will she pay?" It was a Friday cliffhanger.

Most people in the U.S. are a paycheck or two from disaster. I was. I'd become a statistic.

"I don't accept." I closed the account and cut up my card. I was terrified. I'd never been without credit. Credit was a rare thing a generation ago. People used Sears cards to buy appliances but nobody ran their lives on credit. Today, we do.

Something felt wrong with the universe. I was getting terrible offers even though I had excellent credit scores, and everyone wanted to give me more credit—at poor terms. It was time to regain control of my finances.

I traded in my expensive VW diesel for a used Bug. I sold or consigned everything I had of value. I stopped going to restaurants and cooked at home. I skipped shopping. I ate out of the pantry for weeks at a time. I no longer bought expensive gifts for holidays and weddings. I stopped every non-critical cent from going out the door.

But the hardest thing of all: I stopped spending my paycheck on my job.

That's no small feat for a teacher. It's nearly impossible to say no. We provide the very best for students, often on our dime. It's expected.

I said no to prom tickets, dress-down days, making raffle baskets, and department contributions to fundraisers. I didn't go to anything that required me to buy a ticket. I stopped shopping for my class.

I got more than a few scowls for not contributing to everyone's worthy causes, but I was now my own worthy cause.

That was smart decision number two. The bad offers, the variable rate mortgages, the red flags, the "something wrong with the universe"—they were the prelude to the Great Recession.

If you want to know what's happening in the economy, don't watch the news. Go outside. Take a walk. Talk to the guy at the gas pump or the lady at the store. Notice the world around you. As for me, I went running. That's how I knew something big was on the horizon. Every time I went out there were more boarded-up homes and vacant stores and I didn't know why. My instinct was right. I'd stopped spending just in time.

Soon after, the crash hit hard. Big box stores went out of business. Banks foreclosed on homes, leaving them vacant for years. Mortgages were bought and sold so many times buyers couldn't find the right bank to pay. Renters got evicted. There was no place for them to go because better-off people who lost *their* homes took the cheap rentals.

The dominoes fell fast.

I made a commitment to myself. I would recover from my debt by living a simple life centered on people, joy, and experiences. I wouldn't overspend. I'd rebuild. From here on out, my household would run on one salary. I'd keep a zero balance on credit cards. I'd create and grow an emergency fund, and if a second salary returned, it would be for getting ahead and paying off debt faster.

Meanwhile, I'd live well—wanting for and wasting nothing.

And most importantly, I would no longer spend my paycheck on my job.

Teaching was one of the main reasons for my debt. I borrowed tens of thousands of dollars for graduate school to take a job that paid half my corporate salary. Then I spent a large percentage of that pay on my job, all while charging my groceries. I always said, "I'll pay it off later."

"Later" never came.

It never does.

You might be a new or seasoned teacher, a teacher in a low-paying district, or even someone outside of education who's deep in debt. Commit to your financial wellness today.

I was terrified when I cut up my credit card. There was no turning back. The Great Market Crash turned out to be a gift, though. I developed skills I never could have imagined. I wrote my first book and started learning new things. I simplified, decluttered, and sent "teacher guilt" packing.

When I did, I learned this: I didn't need a lot of stuff to be happy. I just needed the right people, activities, and things. I also saw how valuable "teacher skills" are. They earn big bucks outside of academia.

In the end, we closed our original business. We moved to the countryside where we live a simple life. I've realized "success" isn't a number in the bank, it's discovering what I want to get out of life, then making it happen.

When students ask about success, that's what I tell them.

Every disaster is a gift in disguise if I'm busy looking for gifts rather than suffering. That was my biggest lesson of all.

Somewhere in the universe there's a mortgage guy who offered me a subprime loan and a credit card company who sent me a sneaky letter—either of which would have ruined me.

I'm grateful for both. They changed my life, and now I know no better way to live.

LESSONS

- Never plan for good fortune to pay off loans. Even "a sure bet" is a Vegas gamble by definition.

- Never rely on credit to pay daily expenses or debt. If you're even thinking of this, break the cycle now.

- Don't plan for a bump in the road. Plan for several.

CHAPTER TWO
The Money Plant

"These… food stamps don't buy diapers."
—Eminem, Lose Yourself

My parents had a financial crisis when I was little. I didn't notice the struggle, though. I only saw the fruits and vegetables. They had a friend who worked at a grocery store. He brought over dented cans headed for the trash. Most had no labels.

It was my job to pick one for dinner. I shook the cans and guessed the vegetable. I could score a big win—peas or corn—or end up with a lima bean defeat. That was the year of welfare.

Dad quit his banking job so my parents could start soup kitchens and set up a group home for adults, but they got left holding the bag instead—an 1863 Victorian mansion bought with their savings. It was on the outskirts of a mill town where no new people come and nobody ever leaves.

My brother Dan and I liked the house. It had a front hallway big enough for a kickball game and a banister we could climb if Mom wasn't around. There were all sorts of nooks and crannies for hide and seek—servants' quarters, walk-in pantries, cupboards, a root cellar, and a front and back staircase that turned the house into a giant loop. There was a barn with three stalls, a tack room, and a hay loft where I found treasures like bottles of nitroglycerin, check ledgers showing bail payments, and a sharpened bayonet. The carriage house under the barn didn't have a carriage, only a broken wheel.

The house oozed history; it was a stop along the Underground Railroad. Slaves hid behind a fake panel in the root cellar on the way to freedom. The three-seater outhouse (connected to the kitchen by a breezeway) was very possibly the first indoor bathroom in town.

"Can we have a horse?" I asked Mom. We needed something to put in the barn.

"No," she said. She always said no to pets. We never did get a new cat after mine got squashed on the road, but at least the house came with four bats in the attic. They added up to one kitten, except they slept during the day when I wanted to play.

Still, I visited them until Mom saw them and put bats on the no-pet list, too.

The house never became a group home. It was a white elephant that sucked away my parents' savings and took a couple of years to unload in a deep recession.

During this time, Dad got a job an hour and a half away at an upscale grocery store close to my grandparents and Paul Newman. It was a temporary job while he interviewed for banking jobs again. He said he sometimes made sandwiches for Spanky of the Little Rascals. Dad stayed with Grandma and Grandpa during the week, and on Fridays, he came home with bags of unsold produce—expensive things like pineapples. They were a big treat.

Welfare's a curious thing. It pays for food—candy even—but not soap or toilet paper. Mom saved cash for those things. It's OK for teens to pay for gas with quarters, but not so cool when you're an adult.

But we had nothing to worry about. We had a magic plant

that grew 20-dollar bills.

I took excellent care of that plant. I watered it, picked off the dead leaves, and checked it every day. I waited for another crop of twenties to grow, then I'd bring them to Mom.

As an adult, I discovered the plant wasn't growing twenties. My parents' friends hid money in it to help out. The magic wasn't in the plant, it was in having a good group of friends.

As a kid, I thought welfare was the best thing ever. Free groceries! Since they were free, I made requests. "Can we get M&Ms?"

"No," Mom said. She always said no.

Welfare may be a 10-year-old's dream, but it's a parent's nightmare. The *riipppppppp* of the coupon book echoed throughout the store—the sound of welfare. People judged. Were we wasting taxpayer money? Were we getting…M&Ms?

Today, getting help is more dignified. Food assistance has credit-style cards. Back then, it was a cardstock booklet that made a distinct sound when the cashier ripped out the coupons one by one.

I'm the adult now. I understand what happened. My parents took a leap of faith that didn't work out. They got taken advantage of, and they had to start over by any means necessary, even if it meant my banker dad taking a job stacking fruit while my mom took care of us alone all week without a car.

I appreciate how difficult it was for my parents to rebuild because I'm rebuilding now. My parents turned struggle—dented cans and expiring produce—into treats and games. We always had what we needed. At the time, I didn't know those years were difficult. I was busy being a kid.

That's the secret, the one my parents lived and the one I know now: *You have what you need. Now, let it bring you joy.*

CHAPTER THREE
Creating a Vision

"When your values are clear, making decisions becomes easier."
—Roy E. Disney

"You have what you need. Now, let it bring you joy."

What does "living a good life" mean? What things and experiences do you want?

It's tough for teachers to answer because we usually want things for others, not ourselves.

I would've said, "Enough money and a good job." But words like "good," "bad," and "enough" don't paint a picture. Without a crystal-clear vision, I was stuck.

I was treading water, making no progress, because I didn't have a vision.

Begin by Creating Your Vision

"What do you want?"

I didn't know, so I asked myself a question. "If money wasn't an obstacle, what would I do? What experiences would I choose? What would life look like?" I knew what I *didn't* want—I didn't want to search plants for cash and guess my dinner by shaking cans. I didn't want to worry about bills and debt. I made a list of things I didn't want. The list grew. And grew.

But there was a problem.

In listing things I didn't want, I was reinforcing the negative, giving it space to stay alive, *preserving it on a list*, and I wasn't getting any closer to creating a vision I could see.

Words matter. They make or break success. I had to convert each "don't" to a "do" in order to know what I wanted rather than what I wanted to flee. Avoiding things is living in fear. Working toward things is building and growth.

I got a new piece of paper and wrote, "Things I want."

I took item one from the old list: *"I don't want to struggle."*

"Then what do I want?" Flip the language. "I want to be financially secure."

I tried to picture "secure." I couldn't. What was it? Ten thousand dollars? A million?

I thought for a while. I realized something. "Secure" is a feeling, not a number. I know millionaires who don't feel secure and I know people with two dimes who want for nothing and are the happiest people on earth.

"I want to pay bills and have enough left over to say 'yes' to reasonable things." That was quantifiable. I knew how much my bills were, and I knew the cost of things I said no to. Check.

I moved on to the next items on the list.

I don't want to be micromanaged.

I don't want to worry about evaluations.

I don't want to hear "no" every time I have an idea.

Many of the things on my list weren't about money at all. They were about autonomy, freedom of spirit, and regaining control.

We joke about these things in education—how everything's scheduled, right down to the 18-minute lunch and the 30 seconds we have to pee. I understand that order is important. But the age of big data brought in something more than order. It brought standardization, testing, and fear.

I don't want to be afraid anymore.

Fear and money are deeply connected, because "broke" is fear's best disguise. I couldn't create a proper vision for how I wanted to live until I first stopped being afraid.

I finished my list.

"I want to say yes to opportunities. I want to buy what I need without obsessing about the price. I want an emergency fund. I want to be debt free—to pay off my student loans, pay off the house early, maybe go on a trip. I want enough money to give to others. I want to be free in all things—wallet, mind, and soul."

That was a list I could get behind.

The next steps: to rank the items in order and break them down into actionable goals.

"Pay off the house early," isn't good enough. Who knows what that means? If there's no plan to make it happen, it won't.

Here's something actionable.

One day, I learned I was $1,300 away from being able to remove PMI insurance from my mortgage. Private mortgage insurance is an expensive add-on to mortgages for certain types of loans or for people who don't make a big enough down payment. I could save a lot of money by paying my loan down enough to get the PMI removed. That $1,300 was all that stood in my way.

I did something I promised myself I would never do: I borrowed money from my "Uncle Sam Fund." That's money I set aside for taxes. That fund is sacred; I never touch it. This time, I made an exception. I paid down my mortgage and got my PMI cancelled. This lowered my payment by $211 a month. I repaid the fund with the $211 I was saving. Then, I tacked it back on to the mortgage payment to pay extra toward the principle.

Doing this cut *six years* off my mortgage and didn't cost me an extra dime. That is an actionable plan to propel me toward my vision of being debt free. Only actionable plans become real.

"Maybe go on a trip." That's never going to happen until I put the dates on the calendar, get a dog and chicken sitter, and go. But I can—once it becomes part of my vision.

My ultimate vision of life was this: *I want to work hard every day knowing I did something good, that I had fun doing it, and that I have enough money in the bank to do it again tomorrow.* That's what it all boiled down to.

Sounds simple, but there was one problem: My life wasn't aligned with my list and vision.

Alignment

Now that I had the list, any thought or action got me closer or pushed me farther away. I began to ask this, "Will this get me closer to the life I want to lead?" In the beginning, the answer was usually "no." I needed to change.

Making a change is like learning a new dance. I have to learn each new step, then practice until it's automatic. "Does this get me closer?" *Go!* "Farther away?" *No.* I asked, answered, adjusted, and acted until my dance became a graceful tango with the person I wanted to be.

When I'm out of alignment, it's not always because I'm backsliding. Often, it's because I've grown. To make progress, I need to leave old thinking behind and move into uncharted waters.

Getting to the Top of the Mountain

Adjusting a decade-old vision I've outgrown isn't easy.

"You need to shit or get off the pot," my mom told my dad. "You've been 'gonna climb' that mountain every year."

Mom was tired of hearing about Mt. Washington. Every spring Dad said he was going to climb it. He brought out the guide books. Every fall he put them away.

One year, Mom told him to either climb the mountain or find a new goal. We climbed Mt. Washington that summer, and we made it to the top. The climb wasn't nearly as difficult as setting the plan in motion.

Goal setting, rebuilding finances, and mountain climbing have a lot in common. Plan for the best and adjust to the reality. Not every climber gets to the top of every mountain. Not every person reaches their goal right away—or at all. That's okay. What matters is the journey, and the progress made along the way.

Elite mountaineers train for years to climb Everest. They take months to prepare. At the basecamp, climbers acclimate for weeks before attempting to summit. Shortcut one single step, overestimate your readiness, or climb with your ego, and you pay with your life.

Here's the difference between world-class experts and amateurs: one quits, the other stays the course.

You might think it's the amateur that quits. The opposite is true. It's the expert. The expert doesn't waste energy on things that no longer serve a purpose. The expert knows to change direction when things fall apart, even if it's heartbreaking to do so.

My friend Andy is a top-level mountaineer. He's a retired Army combat surgeon who literally wrote the book on mountain medicine. He's the guy you'd want with you in an emergency. He's also climbed pretty much every mountain God put in his way.

One year, he went to Denali, North America's highest peak. The guides set up a website for friends to follow along. On Andy's day to summit, the weather didn't cooperate. The group aborted the mission and descended. They never got to the top.

Fifty-percent of climbers who attempt Denali never summit. There's no shame in descending—I have more respect for those who do. Their ability to make that call when the ego says "Press forward..." That is exactly what makes them the best of the best instead of dead.

It's hard for me to acknowledge when a long-term vision no longer serves me. That vision is familiar and comfortable. To stay the course when it no longer makes sense to do so is dishonest— it gets me further from my dreams.

As important as it is to create a clear vision, it's equally important to throw old ones away.

Here's one teacher's story about letting her vision go.

Amy moved to take a teaching job 1,500 miles away from her home. "It was a chance to contribute to a district that really needed teachers," she said. If she asked herself the question, "Will this job get me closer to where I want to go?" the answer would have been yes, initially.

Then, unexpected things happened. Amy's new district took a long time processing her certification. They paid her as a substitute during that time—barely minimum wage. Her new pay was half her old salary even after the error was fixed, and she was denied the signing bonus she'd been promised. Her classes were giant, and the conditions weren't what she'd been told. She began to struggle.

In the beginning, Amy's new opportunity aligned with her vision. Then, things changed.

Like a mountaineer watching the weather, it's critical to notice when conditions change. "Will this get me closer to where I want to be?"

Eventually, Amy said, "No." She left.

Defining and maintaining a vision is hard. Write it down. Commit. Keep asking yourself, "Does this thought or action get me closer or further away?" If the answer changes to "no" or "further away," don't be afraid to change course. It's not failure, it's growth.

The world is my oyster—if I've trained myself to look for pearls. That's what creating vision is all about. Sometimes the pearls aren't where I think they will be. I can't be afraid to pull up anchor and look somewhere else.

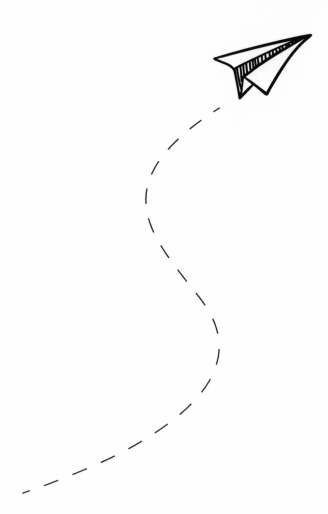

SECTION TWO
Stop the Bleeding

"The way to build your savings is by spending less each month."
—Suze Orman

"Money won't create success—the freedom to make it will."
—Nelson Mandela

Objective

Say "no" to the nonproductive, making room for things of value.

Identify marketable "teacher skills" and use them to make cash.

Instead of cutting from the budget, add to the bottom line.

CHAPTER FOUR
Don't Spend Your Paycheck on Your Job

"You don't help the poor by becoming one of them.."
—Abraham Lincoln

I learned to be poor from teacher movies. They make us think we can fix education with a single pack of loose-leaf paper if only we'd work a little harder.

There are five main parts to a teacher movie: the challenge, the hero, the warning, the butt kicking, and the win.

All teacher movies start with a stereotypical problem—gangs, poverty, a losing basketball team. The hero's either a Polyanna who'll save education or someone climbing from the bottom of the barrel to get back on top.

The hero gets the kids everyone hates.

"Good luck with *them*," someone says. Someone throws a paper airplane as the hero walks in the door.

And so it begins.

The hero gets a Chuck Norris-level butt kicking. Bureaucrats declare victory. At the last minute, the hero wins. Everyone walks off into the sunset, lives changed. Roll credits. That's the teacher I wanted to be—that perfect teacher.

That's exactly why these movies are so dangerous. Because that teacher doesn't exist. You can't save the world by running yourself into the ground or going into debt funding your class.

Let me say that again: *You can't save the world by running yourself into the ground or going into debt funding your class.*

That only works in Hollywood.

One night, I was home alone watching a teacher movie. The teacher in the film got the bad class with no supplies, as expected. She took two jobs to pay for her job. Every kid got a pencil, an A+, went to Harvard on scholarship, and won a Pulitzer Prize. I think one became president and another was elected Pope, but things didn't work out for her. She went broke and got divorced.

"You married your job, not me," her husband said.

I cheered when he walked out the door. *Good riddance! He doesn't appreciate you!*

In the middle of the movie, my husband's Jeep pulled into the driveway. I jumped for the remote and grabbed a book like I'd been reading for hours. Why was I acting like someone doing drugs, watching porn when I was just watching a movie?

I realized...it was because the woman in the movie was me. I was looking in a mirror, and I didn't like what I saw. I didn't want to get caught watching a film where a teacher spends all her cash on her job while feeding her family lawn clippings. *She got two jobs to pay for her job, ended up alone, and that was the happy ending?*

My priorities were wrong. I was on a fast track to disaster. I had to change. I promised myself, "From now on, I'll do less."

"Less?" you ask. "What kind of teacher are you?"

A real one.

I was a 25-hour-a-day teacher for years, spending myself into a hole. "No" wasn't in my vocabulary.

I bought clothing, food, and school supplies for students while racking up debt. I put myself last in line because there was always something to buy or do for school. If I tried to balance myself, someone said, "It's for the kids." Everyone nodded and cracked open their wallets or formed another committee.

Teachers go from "great" to "savior complex" quickly. I've seen lives ruined by this—finances, careers, and families. I was headed there in a race car.

The solution? Learn to say, "No."

It's hard. People were used to my "yes." "No" came as a shock to them. In the beginning, I apologized and caved a lot. Like anything else, "no" takes practice. It's heavy weightlifting and I always dropped the weight on my foot.

"Next time I'll be firm," I promised myself.

It didn't take long for "next time" to come and my "no" didn't make me any friends.

I had to learn to be OK with that.

"I'm sorry, that doesn't work for me."

I was kind. I gave my reasons.

"That's not a possibility."

"Here's a better solution."

Finally, when the conversation got to the point where I usually caved, I said, "No. I'm not going to do that."

I was polite, but firm.

In the beginning, things got ugly, but I survived. I survived conflict, disagreement, and standing up for myself. That was the critical lesson. The world didn't crumble when I said no. I just got a little bit stronger.

Standing up for myself was the right thing to do, but it was only the beginning. The next step was this: to stop apologizing.

The next time I said no, I removed "I'm sorry"—because I wasn't sorry. The person wasn't happy, but I stayed firm.

Finally, I stopped justifying "no" altogether. Not sorry. Just no.

No reason given. I don't owe the world my paycheck or dawn-to-dusk service. And I don't have to explain.

As I learned to say no, people stopped trying to take advantage of me. I could see who my real friends were. "No" helped my budget, but it helped my relationships as well.

If I'm a doormat workaholic spending myself into a hole, I'm not showing students a good example. By being firm and taking care of myself, I model strength and self-respect. Those are two things kids need in this world. Adults, too.

Say No to Classroom Spending

The average teacher spends between 500 and 1,000 dollars in the classroom each year. Teachers buy everything from tissues to hand sanitizer. They feed kids and purchase pens by the thousands. A New York City teacher I interviewed spends 5-6,000 dollars a year on her classroom, then crowdfunds "the big things" like texts. Imagine the position she'd be in with an extra 5-6,000 dollars every year. Instead, she gives herself a double-digit pay cut in an industry that doesn't provide raises.

People usually go to work to get paid. Teachers do the opposite: They give back 10 to 20 percent off the top, then juggle bills. Stop!

School spending started slowly for me. I'd buy one thing on sale and "just one more thing" later. I'd stock cabinets during back-to-school sales. Each little purchase added up.

"I'll pay it off next month," I'd say.

I never did, because something else always happened. Life secret: There will always be "something else." Set a hard and fast "no spending on work" rule and rebuild from there.

Say "No" Without Guilt!

How does a good teacher say no when there are so many needs? Is there a solution?

Yes. There is. Know this: Unless your last name is Gates or Rockefeller, you can't provide for every kid. Accept that or you'll go down in flames. Failing to say no nearly ruined me.

"I'll catch you later, Miss," one student said about her prom ticket, which I'd covered for her. "I get paid on Friday."

Nobody ever caught me later. I paid out of my pocket again and again.

The amount I spent on my job and students would've paid my bills, cleared up my student loans years earlier, or given me the emergency fund I didn't have when the emergencies came.

I was saying "I'll catch you later" to myself. "Later" became my alternate reality.

There is no "later" if you want to build or rebuild your finances. Debt didn't make me a savior. I ended up a martyr instead. Classroom spending is addictive behavior. Recognize it for what it is and avoid it at all costs.

These days, I rarely spend on my job. When I do, it's my choice—no guilt. Some hot chocolate, an occasional treat. When school doesn't provide things, I don't go shopping. I create a Plan B.

"Anyone Who Won't Give Students a Pencil Shouldn't be Teaching"

"Miss, do you have a pen?"

"I have *my* pen." Saying that is nicer than saying "no."

I was chatting with someone on Twitter. He said anyone not

willing to give a kid a pencil shouldn't be teaching. That hit hard, because I'd recently started my no-spending policy. I was making real progress on debt. I didn't want to feel I shouldn't be a teacher because I didn't personally supply my class.

I asked the other person to consider that I have more than 100 students. One year I had 256. Many asked for something frequently. It's what kept me in debt.

"I never said *buy* them," he said about the pencils. He said every school has a test supply cabinet. "Go there and get pencils."

I respect this man, but "go to the test cabinet" doesn't work. Supplies are under lock and key—literally. If a supply cabinet exists, there's definitely a guillotine and minefield in front of it. We get 20 dollars a year to use on whatever we want. Those 20 dollars aren't worth the time it takes to hunt through the thousand-page catalog and fill out the requisitions, and it certainly wouldn't keep me in supplies for the year.

According to the National Retail Federation, America spends 75 billion dollars on back-to-school supplies annually. Most of that was me. I'd start stockpiling in July. I'd go to every store, twice a day, at shift change. I'd match sale fliers to coupons and hunt for a young cashier.

"I know it's 'limit five.' Can I get 50 now? Otherwise I'll be back twice a day, all week, with coupons." A crazy woman with coupons is a teen cashier's worst fear. That's how I got enough supplies to last a decade.

When the financial crisis hit, I had a choice: school spending or food. I chose food. When the school stockpiles ran out, I started saying no.

A funny thing happened when I started saying no. Students came better prepared or shared. They didn't hate me.

"No" was a good lesson for students, but a better one for me.

Wharton professor and organizational psychologist Dr. Adam Grant talks about givers, takers, and matchers in his book "Give and Take: Why Helping Others Drives Our Success." Dr. Grant measures how people's giving style correlates with success. What he found was surprising. "Givers" are disproportionately represented at both ends of the spectrum. They're life's superstars and its doormats. I was a doormat.

How can being a giver make a person *either* successful or unsuccessful?

Dr. Grant says it's simple: The determining factor is how people give. Successful givers are targeted givers—generous but selective. They give to givers and matchers, people who are likely to pay it forward and maximize the gift. They want a return on their investment in giving. Successful givers don't give to excess or give to takers. Unsuccessful givers do both.

I was an unsuccessful giver.

"They're taking advantage of you." Karim, one of my former students, sat me down for a talk. He said students found ways to get things that were important to them, and education needed to be important to them. "You're not the world's Walmart. People in third-world nations have nothing and they fight for education."

He was right.

It's the law of supply and demand. There's only so much to go around—whether it's time, effort, help, or money. When I say "yes" selectively, "yes" has value. Successful giver. If I say "yes" to everything, I'm taken for granted. *Unsuccessful giver.*

Now, when I give or spend, it's from the heart. It has meaning. It brings me joy. It is always my decision, never an obligation. *Successful giver.*

When I learned to say no and put myself first, the rest started to fall into place.

Kill the "I Needs"

I ask overcommitted, overspent teachers why they spend money they don't have.

"I need it for class," is the answer. Or, "It's for the kids." That's a weak justification for destructive behavior. Do this instead:

Replace "I need" with "what if...."

What if...I had no money, but I had to do this?

What if...I could only use things I have or could trade for?

What if...I had to choose one committee?

When faced with great challenges, great people do even greater things to succeed.

What if you weren't allowed to spend your personal money on your job? What if it was against the rules? How would you accomplish the mission?

United States Marines say this: "Adapt and overcome." It works.

Don't confuse needs with wants. There are very few real needs. Ask "what if..." instead.

That was the magic shovel I used to begin digging out of the hole.

CHAPTER FIVE
Making Friends with Money

"I won't spend less. I'll make more."
—Kamal Ravikant, author & entrepreneur

There's a risk to starting on the path to financial recovery. The risk is going to the other extreme. It doesn't happen to everyone, but it happened to me. I battened down the financial hatches until I made Ebenezer Scrooge look like a big spender.

"I'll skip groceries for one more week." I thought of myself as frugal and sustainable, but the truth was this: I was obsessed—borderline insane. That's the wrong approach.

I had to make friends with the concept of money, to learn to use it as a tool. It was an overpriced vacuum and a successful friend's philosophy on cash that helped me learn how.

A few summers ago I visited my friend Liz at her mother-in-law's cabin deep in the Maine wilderness. The kids tracked mud on the newly refinished floors. No one wants a mad mother-in-law, so naturally, I ran to clean. I loved her vacuum—so light, so smooth. I wanted to vacuum more.

"You should buy one," said Liz. "These are great."

It was expensive—way more than I'd ever pay for something that cleans dirt off floors. *My vacuum works fine*.

But this time, instead of making an excuse, I tried something I'd seen my entrepreneur friend Kamal do with great success.

Instead of saying no to things, he does this: he says, "I'll just make more."

Then he does.

I ordered the vacuum.

Is this a spending violation? Should I have put that amount toward reducing my student loan?

To buy or not to buy, that is the question. I'll render a verdict at the end of this chapter.

First, Let's Peek at a Typical American Couple Discussing Finances

"How much do you spend on groceries?" the wife asked.

"Do you know how much credit card debt you have?" the husband fired back.

There I was, stuck in the middle of a family feud. My answers would break the tie. That's a dangerous place to be.

"Yes," I answered. I could account for every cent leaving my wallet. After my no-credit period, I opened a low-limit card and used it to track my purchases.

Many couples have a spender and a saver. The tighter the budget, the worse the divide.

I'm the saver in my family—the miser, really. I pick change off the ground and live like a monk. At times, I go overboard.

"Satellite radio's only 12 dollars a month." My husband wanted to keep a few pleasures as we rebuilt our finances. Meanwhile, I washed out freezer bags and reused dental floss to save a dollar or two.

Things were bad. No one piece of dental floss was going to change that, but I'd already traded in my car, stopped shopping, and Craigslisted anything of value. I was looking under rocks for a few more pennies.

"It's only 12 dollars…."

I added up all the instances of "it's only," the things I'd bought or failed to get rid of because they were "only" a few bucks each. Memberships, subscriptions, and recurring charges didn't seem like a lot—20 bucks here and there. Many I didn't use or forgot about completely.

"It's only 10 dollars."

"It's only a little."

"It doesn't cost much."

Nothing was expensive on its own, but together, the "it's only" list added up to more than 150 dollars a month of complete waste. Small recurring charges are like ninjas—silent and overpowering. Death by a thousand cuts. I canceled them all.

Today, it's not the price of something that influences my decision to buy or keep, it's whether it improves my life in some way. Being able to spend when appropriate—that's what it means to make friends with money.

In a moment, I'll get back to that vacuum.

"I'll Just Make More"

Years ago, I took a second job working with my friend, Kamal. He needed help with some projects. I said yes. Over time, I did more with him until it became a real job with his venture capital fund.

"I think it's a really cool job. You'll like it and you'll learn a lot," he said.

Venture capital? No thanks. I pictured a bunch of Wall Street suits screaming about half-point increases in interest rates. Not my cup of hemlock tea. I didn't realize people with MBAs line up for jobs like these. I only said yes in the beginning because he needed help and no teacher can let a person go un-helped, especially a good friend. It's part of the code.

That's how I got an amazing job by accident.

In the beginning, there was one thing that drove me insane: The budget.

It was my job to keep an eye on things. But I could do more. I was a master of thrift—at school and at home. I saw opportunities to save. "Let's talk about the budget," I said. *He could find cheaper flights, eat at home more, find savings on...*

"No." He cut me off every time. "That's negative energy." I was trying to save cash, yet he was annoyed.

"You're too cheap. Spend some money," he said. "It's important to spend on things you value." He never cut corners on important things, especially things that saved time or increased productivity.

"You 'value' too much. Spend less," I said.

"No need [to discuss the budget]. If I need more money, I'll just make more," Kamal said.

We were at an impasse.

One day we were working and my computer froze. I'd been pushing off replacing it for months—computers are expensive, and as a teacher, I was used to old equipment so I barely noticed the giant beachball on my screen.

Normally, I'd go make a cup of tea while it permaloaded, but we were trying to finish a project. It was now wasting two people's time, not just mine.

"I'll go after school tomorrow and get a new one." I promised. "It's time."

"What are you getting?" he asked.

First, I rattled off the specs for my dream computer. Then I said, "But that's overkill. I'll get what I have now."

"Don't get the cheap one," Kamal said. "Cheaper isn't always better. It'll be outdated and slow in six months. In fact, I'll get it. Pick what you want. Call it a bonus. You need it for work."

It'll be outdated and slow in six months. In other words, don't save a couple bucks to spend a thousand in the long run.

I still have that computer. I'm using it now. I love it. It's lasted years—a solid return on investment.

Here's what he was trying to teach: Spending isn't about money. It's about value. Get fewer things. Get things of quality. Things that matter, last, and bring joy or efficiency. That contributes to a life well lived.

It costs more to lose work time, lose efficiency, and lose joy. Saving pennies costs dollars in the end.

I struggled to spend on the things that mattered because I had a distorted self-image. Many teachers do. I saw myself as a hero spinning society's scraps into gold, someone who could make do in any situation. Kamal saw himself as a skilled entrepreneur who built things and could create the income he needed.

Who was more prepared for growth?

I didn't believe in the philosophy of "I'll just make more" right away. There's no "I'll just make more" fairy for teachers. I continued cutting things out of my budget to survive. While I picked pennies off the ground to make my finances work, Kamal built big things. I watched him do it again and again—from ground zero to the sky.

"I'm going to teach you to do this," he said.

I couldn't imagine making money. That's exactly why I didn't.

After some time, I noticed a pattern. It was no accident I was just breaking even, then going backwards while he was growing. It was the way we saw things. He saw opportunities for growth. I saw opportunities to save. I was limiting myself, shrinking, still living my life on the "don't" list.

In education we say "the sky's the limit" while we remain firmly chained to the earth. We model limiting behaviors every day of our lives: scrimping, saving, cutting things out, saying no. We applaud teachers who do it best.

We get this message from districts and states who spend millions of dollars on "initiatives" while telling teachers to fund their own classes. Thrift and "cheap" are the only things we know—we live in survival mode.

When we behave that way, that's what we teach our kids.

I didn't want my students to learn to be cheap and to pick pennies out of couch cushions for their entire lives. I wanted them to be wise with their money while they learned, "I'll just make more." So I tried to teach it, even while I didn't always believe in the magic myself.

I started to observe what successful people were doing, then do that. "Does this add value?" "How can I make more?" Eventually, it started to work. It's a total shift in behavior.

"I'll just make more" is about removing limits and seeing opportunities. It's hard for teachers—sometimes nearly impossible. It takes a lot of reprogramming.

In my family, extreme self-sacrifice is a badge of honor. Cheap is a virtue that goes back generations. I'd cut out five coupons while my successful friends ate five-star meals.

I started to notice something. Even when we did similar tasks, my non-education friends made much more money for doing them than me.

"Why?" I asked Kamal. People called him all the time for

consulting and advising. When I did similar things—organizing, helping, advising, or consulting—it was called "a favor." He got large checks. I had to check my bank account to see if there was any money left. He was "an expert" while I was "a big help." Experts get paychecks. "Helpful" people get used and abused.

Why the difference?

There were two reasons. The first, he said, was mindset. He didn't feel guilty getting paid what he was worth. I once charged market rate for tutoring and felt guilty for years. Teachers are trained to apologize if we even think about money. To charge is to be greedy.

The second reason was the fields we were in. Education pays less. I noticed this when I began to freelance. Given two similar jobs, the one in education paid half as much—or less—than an equivalent job outside of education. Working conditions were different, too. Education jobs were bureaucratic and wasted a lot of time. Jobs in tech were the opposite. They paid well and respected my expertise.

If I wanted to "just make more," I had to do two things: I had to charge for my value and say "no" in spaces where people expect everything to be free. For teachers, this falls somewhere between a mind shift and a career change.

But if I learn to recognize my value, I can increase the bottom line instead of cutting everything out until the budget works.

Can I Buy It?

Earlier, I asked if the vacuum was a spending violation. Should I have skipped the purchase?

I tried "I'll just make more" for the first time. I wrote a couple of articles for a company and negotiated a higher rate specifically for the vacuum. It worked!

Adding to the bottom line to get something has the exact same effect as a spending freeze—the budget balances—but it feels a whole lot better. I don't have to be a monk to be responsible with money, I just need to make sure the math works. Then I can leave "broke teacher" behind.

Don't get me wrong, I can still make an empty tube of toothpaste last six months, but I can also go to a restaurant and order off a menu that doesn't have prices listed. I'm more in balance.

The goal is to make more than I spend. I have valuable skills the world needs, and the world is willing to pay me for them if I ask instead of volunteer. "I'll just make more" helped me believe this and make friends with money.

I promised my wallet I wouldn't leave her empty again.

CHAPTER SIX
The "B" Word

*"The budget is not just a collection of numbers, but an expression
of our values and aspirations."*
—Jacob Lew

The "B" word. Budget. Everyone hates it. It's as bad as the "D" word—diet.

People on diets are always miserable. Vegans, carnivores, paleo, keto, keto paleo, ketopaleovegetarian, gluten free, kosher, and Whole 20…they look mad at every dinner party. The vegans protest the steak, the paleo and keto folks sniff at dessert, and the kosher guy whips a matzo from his pocket and nibbles in the corner.

"Hooray! I'm eating carrots and broccoli!" said no one ever. A good diet is a positive, healthy lifestyle, not a plate of garnishes rejected by an angry French chef. It should bring pleasure, but it doesn't, so people cheat. Fake bacon, sugar substitute, keto bread, paleo brownies…. Show me a caveman who ate brownies.

Budgeting is the same. People know it's good for them, but they're miserable so they cheat. "It's only 10 bucks." Game over. You lose.

It's never the big things that get you. Nobody eats an entire cheesecake and gets fat, just like nobody buys a mansion on the way home from work and goes broke.

But you will buy a coffee, hit up a Walmart sale, go to happy hour, stop at the grocery store for one thing and spend a hundred dollars, click "purchase" online, or go out to eat because you haven't planned dinner.

It's the 365 times a year you spend an unplanned dollar that keeps you from reaching your goals.

"Budgets don't work for me."

Yes, they do. Always. If you obey them. People don't because they're set up like a giant list of "No!"

Your budget should be the plan that gets you to your list of dreams. Tracking expenses is critical. Otherwise, you'll never see cash walk out the door. Here's a typical month of untracked spending:

Coffee on the way to work: $80 a month.

A trip to Walmart for "a couple of school supplies on sale":$70.

Unplanned takeout four times: $120.

Shopping while hungry: $50 a week extra.

Impulse purchases online: $100 a month.

See how easy it is to blow through an extra $570 on things that don't matter? That's more than $6,842 in potential savings in just one year.

I'm not saying skip purchases, I'm saying if it's a priority, write it into the plan. My budget lets me see when my money tries to sneak out the back door so I can send it where I want it to go.

Kamal was right when he said my budgeting brought negative energy. It wasn't the budget, though, it was me. I wasn't budgeting, I was obsessing.

Fear attracts the things we try to avoid. I learned this studying Japanese sword. Every class, I'd get hit.

Don't get hit, don't get hit, don't get hit...whack!

I practiced harder. I still got hit. My instructor finally spoke.

"Think of what you're going to do, not what you don't want to happen," he said. "What's the end result you want to achieve?"

Think of what you're going to do, not what you don't want to happen.

This works for all things, especially budgeting.

Think of the things budgeting allows you to have instead of what you must cut out to get there. That's how to rebuild with a smile.

I was reading posts on a frugal forum. There was a mother of nine who was spending too much at the drive-through while running her kids around. Her daily Coke and sausage biscuit added up. People told her to stop drinking soda and eating fast food so she could save money. They assaulted her with the health benefits of lettuce and water.

That's not what this is about! Budgets are judgment free. Create your vision and find a way to make it happen.

I told the mom to buy a few cases of Coke on sale. Then prep and freeze sausage biscuits at home. Heat one up, grab a can, and go.

I've done this myself, only with coffee.

"You got a 20-dollar mug?" my husband asked.

"Yup." I said. It's a nice Yeti mug. I've had it for years. It's the first mug I haven't lost or destroyed, and it keeps my coffee hot. I get the best coffee I can and I brew it at home. I save hundreds of dollars and my coffee's perfect every time.

Find a way to have the exact things that make you happy in a way you can afford. Don't cut corners when it matters.

How to Make a Realistic Budget

Budgeting isn't a straight journey. It's a two-steps-forward-one-step-back trip with plenty of setbacks. If you mess up once in a while, tweak the numbers and press forward. You'll get to your goals if you do.

If your budget isn't working for you, there's a reason. It could be that you have a "don't" list that makes you feel like you're in prison camp. If that's your problem, flip the language so it's positive. You should feel you're moving toward something exciting—that you'll get or accomplish it if you stick to the plan. Whether it's paying off a credit card, saving for vacation, or buying something big, your hard work must get you closer.

If budgeting still doesn't work, it could be that your budget is incomplete. This happened to me. I couldn't figure out why I kept running out of money. I was forgetting the "occasionals" like propane, home repairs, oil delivery, car registration, and other random expenses that aren't in the regular monthly rotation.

Finally, make sure you have a realistic budget. Many people create a savings or rebuilding budget that's doomed from the start.

"Grocery budget: 30 bucks."

I've done that before, but that's not going to work for most people unless you really know your way around a dry pantry or you don't eat much.

On my budget, I have a column for long-term debt. I keep a running total so I can see how much I've paid it down. It motivates me.

Make a realistic and positive budget. Then follow it. It is your best friend.

When Temptation Strikes

It's easy to backslide. Experts have all sorts of tricks to

defend against this. They tell people to journal, remove spending apps from phones, use cash, or freeze their credit card in a block of ice. None of this works for me.

Cash only? I'll get more at the ATM.

Remove apps? Amazon's accessible on my browser.

Journal? Logging every penny just makes me obsess in the end.

Block of ice? Seriously?

I can defeat any gimmick. There's one thing I can't defeat: honesty. *"Does this get me closer to my goals?"*

Anything less than honesty sells me out. What's the real issue here? I identify it. I get back on track.

Fixing my budget was like putting a Band-Aid on a gunshot wound. It was difficult on a good day and hopeless all the rest. I'm learning to dust myself off more quickly and get back on the path.

It's never a straight line to my dreams.

But that's part of the adventure.

CHAPTER SEVEN
The 500-Year Flood

*"The best time to plant a tree is twenty years ago.
The second-best time is now."*
—Chinese proverb

Budgets and financial plans only work if you've got money coming in. One week I got an email saying I didn't get paid.

"This morning, it was brought to our attention that a large portion of employees did not receive their payroll direct deposits. Our team has been working quickly to try to resolve the issue. Despite our best efforts today, you are among a small percentage of employees whose direct deposits will not be deposited until Tuesday."

I almost deleted the email. The subject line said, "Questions, ACH."

It should've said, "YOU'RE BROKE! STOP SPENDING!"

I shifted money from the emergency account to the account that pays the mortgage. Problem solved.

"We regret any inconvenience this causes you. We will cover the costs of any overdraft fees incurred from today's payroll delay."

I didn't have overdrafts; the emergency fund did its job. But the fact I had to shift funds to cover one missing paycheck means I wasn't out of the danger zone yet. I still had a lot of improving to do.

Would one missing paycheck put you in a bad position? If so, you're not alone. Much of America is in this exact same spot, and it's getting worse.

According to a January 2015 report by the Pew Charitable Trusts, the majority of Americans are not prepared for the smallest financial blip. The Washington Post reports a staggering 46 percent of households couldn't cover a 400-dollar emergency expense if they had to. That means they don't have the cash, credit, or anyone to call for that amount.

Most of the nation has only two weeks of emergency funds instead of the recommended three to six months.

"Even when pooling all of its resources—including from accounts that are potentially costly to access, such as retirement accounts and investments—the typical middle-income household can replace only about four months of income," the Pew report says. The exact number is 119 days.

I liquidated my first job's 401(k) in my late twenties "to pay down debt and get ahead." That was stupid. I paid a ton of tax penalties and burned through what would've been a fairly sizable sum today. Then I created more debt because I felt like I had breathing room. That's what happens.

Getting out of debt isn't a one-time reset button, it's a way of life—like training for the Olympics.

Elite athletes do their workouts, they say no to beer and parties, eat like champions, go to bed early, and push limits again the next day. Every minute of every day is related to the goal. It's not an impossible journey. It's a long one. The winners win by never giving up in the face of setbacks and overwhelming odds. They dust themselves off and get back in the game. The same is true with financial rebuilding.

Are You Flying in the Danger Zone?

Things can get rough. Having no cash reserve isn't just unwise, it's dangerous. We're in a state of income volatility we haven't seen for a long time. The economy's not only changing, it's been blown to smithereens. Nearly half of American households can expect to see a raise or drop in income of more than 25 percent in any given two years.

Pew labels 50 percent of families "income-constrained," meaning they spend an amount equal to or greater than what they earn. Eight percent are "debt-challenged," a nice way of saying their debt is more than 41 percent of their total income.

If you're this financially unstable, one small thing can break you. Today's missed paycheck, tomorrow's illness, car repairs, or near-roof collapse can be devastating, setting you back months or even years.

"The 500-Year Flood" that caused me to learn to lay wood floors was named because even Noah couldn't have predicted it—we weren't in a flood zone. When the Weather Channel's world-famous meteorologist Jim Cantore came to my neighborhood, I knew I was in trouble.

Rhode Island's Pawtuxet River crested 15 feet above normal, cutting the state in half. If I hadn't left work early, I would've been stranded north of that line for days. On the way home I saw two-story buildings swallowed up. For once, Rhode Island made the national news for something other than corruption, potholes, and bad drivers.

We spent the next two days bailing the downstairs with five-gallon construction buckets and a rigged-up Shop Vac, trying to save our furnace. A new one was 5,000 dollars I didn't have.

"Aww, honey," said the girl across the street. "Take a break. I lost my heater. Just use your 401(k)."

I didn't have one. I kept bailing.

When I returned to work a couple of days later, I got a call from human resources. "You have to use personal time if you weren't sick." The governor called a state of emergency and the highway was closed; I couldn't have made to work without a canoe. I had months of unused sick time but only one of my three "personal days" remaining. I had been out two days.

"I was sick," I said.

"Sick" was true. I was sick of water, sick of bureaucracy, and sick of being afraid. I fought hypothermia while bailing and ended up with a two-week migraine. I should've called in sick for the whole two weeks.

I kept my pay.

Many American households are as fragile as blown glass. When one or two days of lost pay can break you, it doesn't get more real than that. No one plans for Depression-level economic collapses or biblical floods. That's why it's so important to start planning for exactly that.

"What's the best time to plant a tree?" the old proverb asks.

"Twenty years ago," is half the answer. I like the second half.

"What's the second-best time?"

"Today."

I will plant my tree today.

Take small actions daily, every day, and you will get wherever you want to go. Just a couple of years ago, one missed paycheck would have been as much an emergency as saving the $5,000 heater was during the flood. This time I simply moved some cash. Next time, I'll have money to spare.

Spend consciously. Save judiciously. Build consistently.

Plant your tree today.

CHAPTER EIGHT
Rebuilding

*"Success isn't always about greatness. It's about consistency.
Consistent hard work leads to success. Greatness will come."*
—Dwayne Johnson

I noticed several distinct stages while rebuilding my finances. The first was the crisis—the moment I knew I was in deep trouble. I panicked. I imagined myself living in a box. I was terrified.

Fear does one of two things. Uncontrolled, it swallowed me whole. Controlled, it lit the fire I needed to fix my problems. I used to picture the worst, then try to fend it off at all costs. Now, I pause. I think about what I want to happen instead of the worst that could happen. Then, I take one small action to get there.

That subtle shift makes all the difference.

A crisis seems like the end of the world, but it's really an opportunity to get back in control. It's triage time.

How much money's coming in? What needs to be paid now? What can I negotiate, punt, save, or cut?

Look for the problem.

"I bought this for class" wasn't the problem. For me, it was this: "I'm overspending because I'm afraid I won't have enough for my classroom, so I stock up." I did this both with school supplies and coupon items at home. I was also giving more in charity and gifts than my budget allowed. I felt like I had transitioned from my corporate income to teaching pay, but the truth was I really hadn't.

Identify the issues. Call them out. Now, take a deep breath. It's time to rebuild.

I stopped spending, switched to DIY mode, and restarted the emergency fund I'd left empty. I only had a few dollars each week to contribute, but I did so. Consistently.

"That's stupid," you're saying. "The emergency fund should be there *before* the emergency." That's true. It's far better to have money available to pay the mechanic when the car breaks down than to wonder how many weeks of groceries I need to skip to rebuild a transmission.

My grandmother always said this: "Put a dollar in the box." She gave me an empty blue bank check box and told me to put a dollar in it each time I earned 10. I didn't understand at the time, but that's a solid 10 percent savings plan—one most adults don't have.

As a teen, I babysat. I put any singles I got in the box, and sometimes a five or a 10. I brought the box to college. It held my waitressing tips. It saved me a couple of times.

I still have the actual box, but today I use an adult version of the concept—an overflow savings account in another bank that doesn't mix with my normal checking. Most experts recommend having a thousand dollars put aside for emergencies, then tackling debt, but I like to have much more.

Why?

Because no emergency in my life ever cost me only a thousand dollars. My emergencies are big. Surgeries. Double-digit tax bills. Unexpected leaks. Roof repairs. You name it, it's more than a thousand. I just had an $18,000 roof situation. What I thought was some peeling paint in a couple of rooms that I'd fix when I got around to it turned out to be five rooms' worth of interior damage from a mystery roof leak. My roof wasn't scheduled for replacement for 15 years. Insurance is paying about half. That leaves me with way more than $1,000 to pay out of pocket.

At the very moment I was texting the roof guy, a tree crashed through the window where I was sitting. It landed six inches from my face. I wasn't upset at the near-death experience; I was thinking about the extra $550 I'd need to replace the window.

Show me a cheap emergency, and I'll jump for joy.

My goal: to have a solid six months to a year of living expenses for emergencies, then additional funds tucked away in investments that can be shifted easily enough if need be.

It all starts with putting a dollar in the box. Then five, then 10, then another 10. I discipline myself to save first, even if it's only a little bit.

That means eventually it'll be there to give to the mechanic, doctor, roof guy, plumber, or whoever comes knocking at the door first.

Recovery

After the initial financial crisis was over, I set up two funds. First, I created a real emergency fund, not a symbolic one. I scheduled payments to it as if it were a bill. Then I set up a splurge fund. I added a few bucks each time I got paid. This is important.

I'd turned into a cheapskate. Having a splurge fund wasn't about blowing money, it was about learning to treat myself well. If I truly believed in my value and in "I'll just make more," I shouldn't have a problem spending once in a while. The splurge fund was to remind me not to be afraid.

Over time, I had accrued a little in the bank. I was freelancing—and charging. I felt comfortable spending a bit more and stopped the extreme DIY. At this stage of the game, doing everything myself was no longer worth my time—or wise, as I saw with the roof damage. Sometimes it's best to let the experts do their jobs.

Author and entrepreneur Tim Ferriss wrote about this in his blog and bestseller "The Four-Hour Workweek." He calculated his average hourly earning potential against what he'd pay to outsource certain things. He found it cost him money to do routine tasks since he could make far more money working with that time. DIY isn't the best option if I could be doing things I do best while paying others to do the same.

Here's an example: In 2010, a flood destroyed the bottom level of my house. At the time, I had zero cash and we were trying to move. If we left the house damaged, we'd take a big hit on the value of the home. We couldn't afford to do that, so I rebuilt the downstairs myself. I learned to lay flooring. I put in trim and painted. I hired people for the plumbing and electrical. The house sold, breaking even.

Today, I evaluate DIY. If it makes more sense for me to do something, I will. Otherwise, I hire someone. There's a tipping point where DIY is just silly.

Curveballs

When things are going in the right direction, something always happens. It's the nature of the universe. When I originally wrote this chapter I was making progress rebuilding, building real momentum.

Today, as I'm editing the final draft, not so much. Life threw me a couple of curveballs.

I'm used to curveballs; I dealt with the roof disaster like a champ. The emergency fund did its job. "See?" I thought, "Do these things and eventually you'll be in a better place." *This works*.

And I *was* in a better place. The sacrifice was starting to pay off.

But there are some curveballs even emergency funds can't handle—the tail end of the last of our business problems. Small businesses struggle; it's the nature of the beast. It's a tough economy and anything can happen. By using our philosophy of "run on one" salary, I could make it work on my end if things got ugly on the business' side.

Sometimes it's not that simple.

Owning a business crosses over the "whose business is this anyway" line into the entire household. I am one half of the household. I'm at real risk of the "I'll just make more" philosophy backfiring, where the "more" would be sucked into a vortex of debt. There's a very real possibility that all my hard work and progress could be wiped out in the process; I'm waiting to see where the chips fall.

None of this is normal teacher stuff—it's a part of business life. The victories are big, but the defeats? Soul-crushing.

There's a reason I think this is important enough to share. I'm rewriting this section on the eve of my final edit being sent to the editor, in the middle of a chapter on rebuilding.

Because if I left it out, I wouldn't be telling the truth. I've been talking about going from financial crisis to momentum and rebuilding to success.

But the truth is this: It doesn't always go that way. And when my stone starts rolling back down the hill I have to be ready to push it back up again. No matter what.

You might not have a small business. You might be tempted to dismiss this part. Don't. My small business might be your medical expense. Or taking care of a family member in need. Or some emergency so far off the radar you couldn't have planned ahead—just when you're seeing the hard work you're doing here pay off.

If that time comes, do this. Breathe. Stand strong. Reassess. Push that stone back up the hill. Eventually, we'll all reach the top.

The major lesson is this: Success is a marathon, not a stroll through the park. The people who succeed are the ones pushing the ball forward, up the field, no matter what.

It's time for me to snap the ball.

Again.

Plan B: sit down and think about each setback I've defeated before. Then take this setback—the real one, not the beast I'm creating in my mind. I'll break it down into conquerable goals.

Then, I'll defeat it in small, actionable chunks. remembering this: *You have what you need…now let it bring you joy.*

And this: *It's a marathon. Take a step. Climb the mountain. Plant your tree today.*

Whatever it takes, that's what I'll do.

There's a book I read years ago called "Three Feet From Gold." It's the story of the Darby family, who bought a gold mine, failed to find gold, quit mining, and sold it. The new owner found gold after digging only three feet.

The Darbys quit three feet too soon.

I won't be a Darby.

Success

I originally defined success as having enough money so I wouldn't stress. Through this latest rebuilding setback, I realized something. It's not that. Success is about learning to build more any time I need to, and to be grateful and content with the things in my life while still reaching for the sky. Success is the power to make things happen.

My idea of success evolves along with my goals. Goals and dreams never stay the same—they are flowing, changing. I never cast my dreams in stone. Dreams are more like the clouds, blowing in and out with each day and season.

To me, success is no longer an amount, it's about finding peace.

CHAPTER NINE
Waste Not, Want Not

"Eat your dinner. Children all over the world are starving."
—My mom

"It either goes to waste or it goes to waist."
—Kristina Cashman

What if you had an extra couple thousand dollars in your pocket right now for anything you wanted? You might—if you didn't waste. Waste costs big and steals opportunities. Eliminate it! Be careful, though. "Frugal" and "obsessively cheap" are first cousins.

I used to feel like the Sultan of Savings because I brought my reusable coffee cup to work. Then, I took "The Waste Challenge." The amount I was still wasting was shocking. Try it. You'll see. You waste more than you think. Every bit of waste you eliminate is a dollar more toward reaching your goals.

The Waste Challenge

Go through your house right now. Look for things you haven't used in the last month or two. Make a list. Search the bathroom, kitchen, basement, bedrooms, family room, attic, woodshed, storage areas. List anything from half-used shampoo bottles to leftovers rotting in the fridge. Skip seasonal items. If you've got skis and it's June, fair enough, but if you didn't use them last winter, on the list they go!

Add up the value of everything you found. The amount may shock you. You could've bought something you really wanted instead.

Most people waste more than they think. Waste isn't only tossing leftovers into the trash. It's hanging onto anything longer than necessary. This includes possessions, time commitments, activities, and unproductive relationships.

Waste is sneaky. It's often disguised as something else—as learning, passion, or opportunity. A forgotten hobby. An unread book. A big part of rebuilding is preventing waste because waste could've been resources used to reach our goals.

To avoid waste, I ask the question, "Does this get me closer to where I want to go?" I avoid getting overcommitted, overwhelmed, and overspent.

Here's an example: I saw a longbow in the store. I got the sudden, uncontrollable urge to practice archery again. I haven't shot a bow in decades.

The bow I wanted was a bit under 500 dollars. It was the kind Robin Hood would've given Maid Marion for her birthday. I live in the country. There's plenty of space to set up a target.

Stop right there!

Time for the question, "Does this get me where I need to go?" *I don't know. Maybe.*

"Maybe?" Time for some follow-up questions.

"Will archery be something I practice long term?" *No.*

"Am I protecting people from the Sheriff of Nottingham?" *No.*

"Are there outlaws here?" *Not usually.*

"Will I be eating Bambi's mom?" *No way.*

"Do I live off the grid?" *I want to, but there's a store down the road. I go there. And I'm a vegetarian. Vegetarians don't hunt for lettuce.*

"Does this skill somehow improve me?" *Maybe. It's very meditative. It improves focus and clears the mind.*

"Will I have time to practice so I can be the best I can be?" *Not a chance.*

Not even one yes. There's the answer. I didn't buy the bow.

I loved archery as a teen. Now, it would be little more than a party trick for a person who doesn't party. I'd have another expensive hobby in my basement. I walked away.

Escaping temptation takes constant vigilance and self-awareness. The "I needs" are logical and strong. "Make her click"—Amazon sends packages to the door.

So I asked "the question" before I bought. "Does this get me closer to, or further away from, my goals?"

No Bambi. No sheriff. No outlaws. No purchase.

"No" was the right answer there, but sometimes I can't shake the urge. I fixate.

Is there a solution?

Yes. The List.

When I have sudden thoughts, or ideas—most of which cost money and time—I put them on The List. The List keeps track of things I want to learn or do. I dump things on the list to clear them from my mind. I can go back to them later. I put archery on the "to learn" list.

Just because something's on The List doesn't mean I have to go shopping. There are creative ways to avoid shelling out cash. For archery, I can spend 20 bucks renting equipment at a local range instead of hundreds on gear to own.

"The Waste Challenge" isn't about self-denial, it's about awareness. I let go of the past to make room for the future.

I've had many passions—fishkeeping, Japanese swordsmanship, martial arts, competition bodybuilding, running, writing, stained glass, calligraphy, homesteading, food preservation, brewing, Japanese calligraphy, sumi-e painting, dog training, music, and photography. I still love some of those things, but others fizzled over time. I kept equipment "just in case."

"Just in case" is a poor excuse. I can always get those things again if I want, but I usually don't. Letting go frees me for other things.

It's easier to declutter when I can find someone with similar hobbies. I gave my fish tanks to Jamie, a fish-loving college student. I sold my stained-glass equipment to artists. I donated the antique china I never used, and I boxed up all my best history books for Kevin, one of the most amazing teachers on the planet. Little by little, I'm letting go. I don't need things "just in case." *I have what I need. Now, let it bring me joy.*

I started getting rid of waste slowly—avoiding it by skipping one "just in case" purchase, stopping back-to-school shopping, giving away one unused thing, and saying "no" to one unnecessary obligation.

Nothing bad happened.

I did it again. Nothing bad happened.

And again. See the pattern?

Tomorrow I'll do it again.

It takes practice.

When I get rid of waste in my life, I become free. I make room for things, experiences, and people I value.

How much waste did I find?

On my waste hunt challenge, I found about 70 dollars of

organic garden pesticides and fertilizers improperly stored. Carelessly stored tools, ruined, cost about 150 dollars. I found unworn clothes (bought on sale) including two pairs of boots a half-size too big. "I'll wear big socks," I remember saying. I never wore the boots.

Things got worse in the kitchen and pantry: expired cans; unlabeled, freezer-burned food. For want of a label, the harvest was lost. Every bit of waste adds up.

Where does America waste?

The kitchen is one of the biggest waste crime scenes in America.

The average household wastes a quarter of the food coming in the door. It's worse in factories and fields—up to 40 percent spoils—and that number is low compared to other parts of the world because we have some of the best agricultural technology in the world. Still, when 25 percent of all Americans don't know where their next meal is coming from, that's unacceptable.

For me, it starts in the garden. "If they didn't want me to plant 50 plants, they wouldn't give me 50 seeds," I say. I overplant every year.

"You're going to waste," my husband says.

I like to plant. To solve this problem, I share with friends, preserve food in season, and store food properly so I don't have to throw it away.

Understanding grocery stores helps me reduce waste and eat better. Sale cycles run every six weeks to two months. I used to stock up during sales, then all the food expired. Now, I buy less— only what I'll use until the next sale—if I go into the store at all.

America's developed a whole culture of waste. We buy

the newest and best, regardless of whether our things are still good. We trade in and trade up. Our global economy depends on continuous spending and consumption. If we stop, industries collapse. Because of this, manufacturers design things to break sooner. What's the point of building quality things if everyone buys a new one every year?

I watched a documentary about "freegans." These are people who try to live free off America's waste. One girl picked her groceries out of a dumpster, and another got small appliances from the trash.

"You can eat expired food...it's perfectly safe," the freegan said.

You might not dumpster dive, but the fact you could shows how much the nation wastes. The same food that ends up in dumpsters in America goes to shelters and soup kitchens in Italy and France. It's the law.

We can do better. I used to belong to a group that brought leftover bread from bakeries to shelters at the end of the day. My California friend Hillary goes to "gleanings," where volunteers pick produce from public lands and donate to the needy.

My dining room table was junk refinished by a local artist. It's beautiful. Some communities teach people to fix household appliances to keep them out of landfills. Older consumer electronics are built to last. They'll run for a century if you give them TLC. My friend Jen's KitchenAid mixer was manufactured in the early 1960s. She cleaned and overhauled it, and it's still working today.

Watching freegans and the zero-waste community in action made me realize I can do better. I can repurpose, reuse, cut back on excess, and share—elegantly. It not only helps the planet, but my wallet, too.

Procrastination

Procrastination is my friend in delaying impulse purchases, but my mortal enemy combatting waste. Whether it's a meal spoiling on the counter because I didn't put it in the fridge or the sock lost by not folding the laundry, "do it now" saves resources in the end.

The Martyr Syndrome

"Waste not, want not" isn't a perpetual diet. It's easy to get so obsessed with avoiding waste that I deprive myself. Like budgeting, "waste not" isn't suffering. It's a way of appreciating the world for its abundance. I remove things I don't value to make room for things I love. I take care of those things so they last.

THREE QUESTIONS
to eliminate stockpiles and waste:

- Are you stocked up well past when the next sale will be?

- Do you have more of something than you can reasonably use?

- Do you have stuff you don't love or use, like old clothes, hobby stuff, or sports equipment?

Let it go!

CHAPTER TEN
Coupons: The Great Lie

"Free is still a price if it takes time."
—Kamal Ravikant

Couponing is the single worst thing I ever did in my life. It's the great lie. It's expensive and nearly destroyed me. Before I stopped, I had shelves upon shelves of nonsense—two and a half rooms to be exact—all "bought for pennies."

When I factored in time, gas, and effort, the real cost was through the roof.

People congratulated me on my couponing skills. They wanted to be like me. Nobody suspected I was slowly going insane.

Watching a good couponer is like watching a street magician. It's an art to behold, but there's a dark side—obsession. Excessive savings is usually a cover for something more sinister—fear and insecurity. When I see people's victory hauls on Facebook, I want to shout, "Do drugs; they're safer!"

Couponing is a drug—a full-blown addiction. One good haul and you'll never go back to recreational couponing again.

It's especially dangerous for teachers, who are always on the lookout for a good deal.

Uncle Jack and Aunt Nancy came to visit one week, so we

took them to the casino. There's not much else to do in eastern Connecticut unless you want to eat pizza or go cow-tipping, and I'd never harm a cow, so we decided to watch horse racing instead. Uncle Jack put five dollars on a horse for each of us. Mine won.

"Winning on your first race is bad," he said. "Promise never to bet on a horse again." His father was gambler. He knew. I kept my promise never to bet on horses, but he never said not to coupon.

Coupons are worse than casinos because society encourages them. A single coupon during a financial crisis turned me from a normal human to a raging lunatic who knew every price, discount, expiration date, and store sale along with the corresponding coupons from each past, present, and upcoming flier. I didn't have one grocery list, I had six, itemized into sub-transactions optimized by store. If I missed a sale, I became stressed about the savings I lost.

I wasn't saving, though. I was spending.

I should've recognized the problem when I installed floor-to-ceiling shelves in an unfinished downstairs room.

I didn't see a problem. I saw an amazing, fully-stocked convenience store where I could "shop" from the comfort of my own home. I loved sending friends and family downstairs to get a week's worth of groceries. They were in awe. This only encouraged my bad behavior.

With the storage room filled, I'd bring carloads to the family shelter. I donated hundreds of dollars' worth of products to families in need. I loved giving—it felt great.

I also loved watching extreme couponing shows.

"*Those* people are crazy," I thought. They turned their kids' bedrooms into coupon stashes. One girl had to dig through toilet paper rolls to go to sleep. Another lady called a store to order a pallet of sugar cereal she was getting for free with her coupons.

"It's courteous to call ahead," she said.

Five hundred boxes of sugar cereal? "That'll kill you," I said.

Any addiction will kill you.

Couponing is an addiction. For a while, it was mine.

At some point, I started to suspect couponing might be an illness, and that maybe I had it. Not only did I buy multiple newspapers each week for the coupons when I object to paper waste so much I use cloth napkins and pack zero-waste lunches, I was going to each store several times a week, organizing transactions so when the first generated, "Get five dollars off your next purchase," I'd have the second ready to go with all the right coupons to get it free. This is highly obsessive, detail-oriented stuff. It was serious—one mistake and the dominoes would fall.

One day, I heard a voice.

"Stop right there!" It wasn't the usual voice in my head. It was bigger, booming.

It was God.

"Look at yourself!" he said. "What are you doing?"

"I'm saving a ton of cash, Lord." I expected a choir of angels singing my praises. Instead, God seemed mad. I'd asked for help with finances and God sent sales. He should've been proud.

"What do you notice about all these things?" He gestured to my stockpile, annoyed to have left his heaven to point out my hell.

I looked around. Five 10-foot shelves on one side, six eight-footers on the other, two in the door frame, and four behind the door. More squeezed into the laundry room, each organized and full. A bodega...for pennies.

I smiled. "I saved a ton."

"Wrong!" he answered. "Grab onto my robe."

Flash.

I was no longer at home, but on God's couch in the clouds watching reality TV—except the person on the show was me.

I saw my stashes and realized *I didn't use any of those things.* Coupons are for unhealthy cereals, preserved foods, and chemical-filled hygiene items I don't use, serve, or eat. I cook from scratch. I grow food. I use natural products. I'd become one of the TV people I judged.

Coupons hook America on junk while Mother Nature desperately tries to feed us naturally, with love. I'd collected a stockpile I wouldn't use in a thousand years, wasting a tenth of the space in my home—and a lot of money in the process. Even if each item only cost a dime, the cost of the waste was still immense, especially after I priced in the time I spent organizing, the gas I used, and the mental weight of the compulsion to never miss a single opportunity to "save."

I'd given myself a part-time job that paid me in 20-cent products with zero value to me. I would've done better working minimum wage with the time I spent couponing. If I paid full price for everything I actually used, I'd have saved thousands.

Couponing is the great lie and a severe addiction. It's fear and spending disguised as saving. I used coupons to distract myself from my financial crisis. I didn't need cheap stuff. I needed to reduce waste, value myself more, and use my value to make more cash.

"Does this get me closer to my goals?"

Couponing sent me in the opposite direction.

My home stash was just the tip of the iceberg. At school, I had four cabinets, a closet, three filing cabinets, and two desks full of things I'd collected in back-to-school sales. I'd spent an astonishing amount of money stockpiling, one penny at a time—

five-cent this, 20-cent that. I did this out of fear that I wouldn't get the resources I needed.

Living in fear is exhausting. It's being on constant alert, like playing every game on the defensive all season long. Nobody wins playing defense. It's a lifestyle of putting out fires, of poverty thinking. It's the essence of being a broke teacher.

That's what we're trying to stop.

"Now do you see?" God asked.

I did see.

I couldn't gain autonomy in my job by stockpiling. I wouldn't fix the economy by chasing down buy-one-get-two-free toothpaste brands I didn't want. And I wouldn't pay off my debt by buying nickel-and-dime things that would sit on my shelf unopened.

I had to vanquish fear, remove waste, and use my true value to build my bottom line. I quit couponing cold turkey.

At school, I asked the question, "What if I had to accomplish this goal with only the things I have now?"

At home, I stopped chasing sales.

I used the extra time to write, plant, read, and learn new things. I wasn't stagnant anymore; I was growing the skills I needed to "just make more."

The nickels and dimes I didn't spend couponing started to compound and dig me out of the hole. I didn't know yet, but that was the very beginning of rebuilding. I was rebuilding my wallet and my spirit, too.

Saving pennies by spending dollars doesn't work. Trying to control the universe doesn't work. It just made me a little bit crazy.

The things that matter most don't have coupons. Once I realized that, I started to be free of them.

It took my family more than three years to use the last of the bottles of shampoo, tubes of toothpaste, and odds and ends once I stopped couponing, and it took more than six years for my school stockpiles to dwindle to reasonable levels. One day I put the remainder on a table and gave it away.

Now I have room in my life for the things I really want instead.

CHAPTER ELEVEN
Crowdfunding Your Class

"Crowdfunding isn't about collecting money. It's about making something happen with a crowd of people who believe in something."
—Jozefein Daelemans

No more couponing and stockpiling? How will I survive?
Some teachers are turning to crowdfunding.

"I can't expect my principal to pay for this," said Sheena Nelson, a Connecticut elementary educator. "My idea was way outside the curriculum, so I crowdfunded." Sheena uses food and cooking to teach elementary kids about health, nutrition, and science.

She started by setting up an indoor/outdoor farm-to-table garden to expose kids to new foods and healthy eating. Her students became better eaters interested in science and their food supply.

Sheena didn't stop there. She applied for and received a $10,000 grant to pay for a Charlie Cart mobile kitchen for her school. The Charlie Cart enables educators to teach food, nutrition, and cooking right in the classroom. Students learn to take charge of their health. It costs $8,500—something her school could never afford, so Sheena found a way to get it.

Next, Sheena wanted to teach kids how to preserve food and avoid waste. She used Donors Choose, a crowdfunding site for education, to buy a class canner and food dehydrator.

She also has an indoor hydroponic garden where kids can see their food grow. She says she sees incredible results in her students— in their learning, interest, and healthy eating habits. Crowdfunding and grants made that happen.

My neighbor Tasha used crowdfunding to purchase classroom equipment and technology for her special-needs students. She's a librarian now, still using Donors Choose to invest in books, furniture, and media center resources in funding-challenged schools.

I'm conflicted about crowdfunding. In my heart, I don't support it. Teachers shouldn't have to beg moms and friends on social media for donations to fund their jobs, and they shouldn't have to spend their free time applying for grants. It's like giving yourself a second job where you don't get paid. Putting fundraising responsibilities on teachers gives schools a false sense of what the budget should be.

But when I interviewed people for this chapter, the crowd shot me down. Many teachers are in favor of crowdfunding, and they're using it to get things they wouldn't otherwise have. Community members, businesses, and philanthropists are often excited to bring students' dreams to life. Crowdfunding can be community building; it gives citizens the privilege of taking part in America's schools.

Karla, a successful real estate entrepreneur, funds projects on Donors Choose. "I like to donate. I get a tax write-off and I feel strongly about education." She's excited to help.

Corporations fund projects, too. Several times, large donors have funded all the items on Donors Choose. Stephen Colbert has done this, Bill and Melinda Gates have, and most recently Ripple (cryptocurrency) has paid for all the projects on the platform.

In that case, why shouldn't Sheena, Tasha, and you get cool

things for your classroom?

Let's look at how you can put together a successful crowdfunding campaign.

Getting started

Your job is this: Build a campaign that makes people want to share and donate. Then, promote it to the high heavens.

First, you need to choose a crowdfunding platform. Kickstarter and Indiegogo are the largest, but Donors Choose is specifically for teachers.

Kickstarter and Indiegogo tend to be for larger campaigns these days—for starting businesses or big projects. Crowdfunding can be about more than just money. It's can raise awareness or gauge interest in an idea before you put money and effort into it. But if you just need a reading rug for your class, Donors Choose will get the job done.

After you decide on the platform, you should think carefully about the timing. If you launch a campaign in December, for example, it's holiday shopping season, but there's also an audience looking for tax deductions.

Time to change your hat

If you're crowdfunding, you just left the role of teacher and entered the world of Madison Avenue advertising. You're now a copywriter, project manager, and marketing professional all in one. If you really want to succeed, you need to get your campaign to spread.

"I teach fifth grade," you say. "Can I do this?"

You can, and you must.

Teachers already do this every day. You convince school haters to love learning. If you can sell math to life's toughest crowd, you can succeed at crowdfunding. Seventy percent of Donors Choose projects get funded. You will, too, if you do it right.

Five Steps to a Great Campaign

1) *Show compelling need.* Write a clear proposal showing potential donors a real need and a huge return on their investment. Donors want to contribute to projects that matter. Be able to explain—with excitement—how valuable this funding will be for students.

2) *Create a solid but realistic budget.* MacBooks are cool but will Chromebooks work at a much lower cost? Maybe, but maybe not. Cheaper isn't always better. Think through the educational goals, show you plan to respect the funds, then ask for things your students need. Don't "make do."

Donors Choose has a section for retailers and price. Avoid fly-by-night retailers and sales. Sales might be over by the time your campaign is funded. You won't have enough money to purchase the items. Use vendors that stand behind the items. Don't pad the budget, just plan well.

Before you put too much work into your campaign, check with your district. Many have rules about purchases and funding. I once declined a large technology donation due to donation regulations. You'll want to know, "Can I do this?"

Also, find out if the purchases belong to you or to the school. If you change rooms or go to another school, does it go with you? These answers may affect whether you decide to crowdfund at all.

3) *Don't bore, implore!* The best campaigns are interesting. They have professional-quality videos. Ask yourself, "Would I click on this?" If the answer is no, keep working. When you have something your audience wants to read and watch, you're on the right track. If it's something they'll share, you've done your job. Here's an example of a teacher crowdfunding a science station:

Boring: "Help Me Fund My Science Station."

Engaging: "How Sitting in the Corner Cured Cancer."

The first example is bad because it's all about you. Rule number one of marketing: No one cares about you. They care what you can do for them. Show donors your students may advance science for them. Donors will be waiting in line to help.

Never let a word escape your pen without first asking, "Have I shown the benefits for my donors? Would I click and share?" If the answer is no, strive to make that answer a yes.

4) *Make a great video.* Successful crowdfunding campaigns use video. Video campaigns are 70-80 percent more likely to succeed. If you're no video pro, chances are you know a 15-year-old YouTuber with some video chops. Get your crowd laughing, indignant, or energized. Emotion sells. You need people to click, share—and most importantly—donate.

5) *Create a big release.* You've got your video, budget, and description. Now what?

A successful release starts long before you go live.

First, make a spreadsheet with all the people you know. Divide them into three categories: inner circle, friends, and acquaintances. For a small campaign, this may be overkill, but for a large one, this will make or break it.

Write three emails or notes—one for the inner circle, another for friends, and a third for acquaintances.

Your inner circle probably already knows about the campaign, so it'll be a quick heads up—a simple but individual text or call. "Hey, Joe, I'm releasing my crowdfunding campaign Tuesday. Will you share it?"

The "friend email" is for people you connect with regularly but don't talk to every day, "I'm releasing a crowdfunding campaign Tuesday for my class science corner." Include some details and a picture if you can, then ask, "Would you be willing to share this?"

Design one last email for people who may be willing to help but to whom you haven't spoken in a while. "Hey, it's been a while! I hope you're doing well. Here's a sneak peek at the science center I'm building for my class. I'll be crowdfunding. Would you be willing to share on Tuesday? Thanks! I'll send the link."

Notice something? I didn't ask anyone for money. That's critical. Nobody wants another fundraising email. However, many people are willing to click or share as a favor. If you've built the campaign right, some will donate.

A day or two before the campaign goes live, follow up with everyone who agreed to share. Check each person off your spreadsheet. "Reminder: My campaign's going live tomorrow! Thanks for agreeing to share. Here's the link."

On release day, post to social media at times your audience is most likely to be online. Customize pictures, captions, links, and hashtags to each platform—Twitter, Instagram, Facebook, Snapchat, etc. You're running your campaign like a social media pro!

Chat, send notes, and follow up with people. Personalize each email. Never write a "send to all" email. I delete those.

The way you connect makes all the difference in whether people support your campaign. You want people thinking, "She's doing amazing things!" not, "I haven't spoken to her in two years and she wants money?"

Thank people when they post and share. Retweet and share their shares with a thank you and a link. Thank people quickly and publicly at every opportunity. This isn't just the polite thing to do. It also lets donors' friends see the campaign without looking spammy. Donors feel appreciated.

Post pictures and videos of your campaign and project in progress. Tag a few people in each post.

"Here's my class preparing the room for our science corner. Kids are cheering—we're halfway there!" You're keeping people interested, but their friends will see the campaign, too.

If you can write posts or articles, do so. Link your project in. Share the campaign everywhere you can until it's funded—and after. Show items arriving, being unpacked, and most importantly, being used. Show the happy ending. Have students send thank-you notes or make videos showing the materials in action.

Letting donors see the effects of their generosity gives them an excellent feeling and sets you up nicely should you want to crowdfund again. Even if you don't, you're paying it forward by creating a good experience for donors. They may fund someone else's project in the future.

With crowdfunding, the sky's the limit. With a little planning and some hard work, you can turn your district "no" into a classroom "yes" and rally the community around your students.

CROWDFUNDING
made simple:

- **Have a compelling need.**
  Show how your project will change the world.

- **Create a business-style budget.**
  Show you're a good steward of the funds, but plan for everything, like shipping.

- **Write good copy.**
  Crowdfunding is advertising. Write viral headlines and descriptions that will be shared.

- **Add video and photos.**
  A picture is worth a thousand words, but a video is worth a million.

- **Send updates often.**
  This keeps your campaign in the public eye.

- **Thank donors and sharers publicly and privately.**
  Never miss an opportunity to give a shout-out on social media or with a note or email.

- **Show productive kids.**
  Post after-campaign shots of kids in action. Show that happy ending. People remember, and the good feeling spreads.

CHAPTER TWELVE
Own Your Loans:
How to Get Out of Debt in Your Lifetime

"With a strong enough why, any how is tolerable."
—Ed Latimore

Three times I came close to paying off my student loans, but emergencies stole the cash.

"Emergencies" are smart creatures. They're pack animals, lurking in the tall grass, waiting to pounce. Just when you've started making progress—saving a little, getting ahead—they lunge.

For years, I had one goal: to pay off my student loans.

"Why?" asked my friend. "It's cheap money."

First of all, mine aren't *that* cheap—they're between five and six percent interest. By comparison, new car loans are between zero and three percent.

Second, I graduated college in the '90s. I never took a forbearance or deferred my loans. I overpaid *the entire time*.

I've been paying student loans for a quarter century. Enough is enough.

Today's college grads are enslaved by debt. I know people paying $1,000 to $2,000 a month on a 20- to 30-year loan. That's a mortgage payment.

You'd never walk into a Ferrari dealership and buy a car for $300,000 when a $15,000 car would work. That's what we do for college. We congratulate students who go to top colleges they can't afford. We spend money we can't afford on classes for certification and recertification in the name of "lifelong learning."

Student loans can't be discharged or forgiven, even in bankruptcy. It's a crisis waiting to happen—especially for those in lower-paying careers. Avoid excessive college debt by any means necessary. Advise students to do the same.

I was having coffee with a friend.

"I should *not* have gone to an Ivy League grad school *for social work*," she said. Instead, she went to University of Pennsylvania. "If I went there at all, I'd have gone to the Wharton School."

UPenn's Wharton School is where top entrepreneurs go to become millionaires. Social workers and psychologists don't become millionaires.

This year, graduate tuition at UPenn is $72,000 for a two-semester program. My undergrad university's tuition is about $70,000 a year for tuition, books, room, and board. Many students take five years to finish. Schools encourage this. That's $350,000—a 20-year student loan payment of $2,310 a month at today's average interest rate of five percent, or $1,879 a month for 30 years.

Is your degree worth *a third of a million dollars* or could you have gone somewhere else for less and received the same education?

This isn't about ego. It's about math.

"College is an investment." I hear that a lot. These must be people who don't invest, though, because investments are supposed to make money.

Let's look at two students. Student One went to a tier-one

school and paid $350,000, then took a $35,000 teaching job. Student Two went to Stanford for Computer Science (about $300,000 for five years), and got a job starting at $150,000/year.

Student One will never recover that "investment."

I'm not saying, "Don't go to college." I'm also not saying, "Pick careers that make you rich."

I'm saying choose a school whose price and quality match your goals. Tell students to do the same. Value shop like you would for anything else. Look under every rock for a deal. College of the Ozarks is a small Christian college that doesn't allow debt. They give students jobs and financial aid instead. Many colleges off the beaten path have good track records for student aid. The military is a great option, too. ROTC pays for college, military academies are free, and GI benefits include college.

Whether you're recommending colleges, or taking classes toward another degree, ask, "Does this get me to where I want to go?"

I was halfway to a Ph.D before I realized the answer was no.

Also ask, "Can I learn this for less?" Thanks to Google, the answer to that is often yes.

The statistics on American debt are frightening. For many of us, debt starts with student loans. America owes 1.2 trillion dollars in student loans. The cost of private colleges rose 179 percent from 1995 to 2015. Out-of-state tuition at public universities increased more than 225 percent.

Seventeen percent of student loan borrowers are behind on payments. The average borrower owes close to $40,000, yet jobs are getting harder for graduates to find. So what do people do? Get more degrees, get further into debt, and try again.

The student loan crisis doesn't stop with the staggering

amount of debt students take on to work in fast food. NerdWallet's 2015 study showed the average American carries more than $15,000 in credit card debt, too.

Only 40 percent of Americans pay their cards to zero every month—60 percent roll them over. The good news is we're saving more than we used to. The bad news is, it's not nearly enough.

Americans save just 3.6 percent of our income. Compare this to the Chinese, who save from 25 percent to 50 percent per household. We spend on everything. The National Retail Federation estimates Americans spend an average of $630.36 per household on back-to-school shopping, almost a thousand on winter holidays, and $74 per person on Halloween. Then there are birthdays, weddings, and other special occasions that pop up, keeping us broke.

It's taken years, but I can finally see the light at the end of my tunnel. Many of today's students never will. Their debt burden is too great. They'll be forced into jobs they hate or they'll default on their student loans until the government takes action against them.

The average debt burden for an American household is nearly $130,000, or 136 percent of income, including *6,000 per year* in interest on those debts. That's money that should be yours.

Debt wasn't a problem throughout much of American history. People frowned on it. In colonial times, people went to prison for debt. Today, debt isn't considered a character flaw at all. Even the president's been bankrupt several times, and investors use debt to offset taxes. When people are in financial trouble, they don't honor their debt, they negotiate out of it. A creditor would rather take a one-time payment at a loss than nothing at all. It's totally legal.

The best thing to do is avoid unnecessary debt in the first

place, especially debt that doesn't put you in a better place. When times are tough, bad debt often seems the only option. This happened to me. Our business was out of cash. I took a call from a "funding agent."

"We'll find you six to 10 lines of unsecured credit at zero percent interest," said the agent. "About 200,000 dollars. You can convert it to new offers when the introductory periods end."

What did that mean? More importantly, what did that mean *for me?*

In business, there are two ways to get money: Take a loan or find investors. There's no such thing as a free $200,000 dropping on anyone's head.

Here's what the agent proposed: For a $6,000 fee, the agent would find credit cards with zero percent introductory offers and keep track of "the portfolio." He'd remind us when offers were expiring, at which time we were to apply for new credit cards and transfer the debt to them.

He was deliberately vague, making it seem easy and normal. Many would've said yes. For every person that did, this man made $6,000 Googling credit card offers while borrowers were ruined.

People under financial stress are in a weakened state, and the credit industry is intentionally confusing. Understanding credit can save you. Sadly for this scam artist, I understood everything he said.

"Let me make sure I understand correctly," I said. "You want me to open six to 10 credit cards with limits from $10,000 to $50,000 each, then apply for more cards when the free periods expire, but you can't guarantee there'll be any zero percent offers available. Then you want us to pay employees using credit cards. We'll have to make minimum payments on a dozen cards with money from *other cards*, and my personal credit score will be ruined. And you'll charge me $6,000 dollars for Googling credit card offers?"

I ended that call.

Applying for credit cards is free. Anyone seeking to make money on people experiencing financial hardship is dishonest, but anyone advising someone to open six to 10 cards for *$6,000 dollars* is predatory.

Here's what would've happened:

Each credit card company would've done a "hard pull," or formal inquiry about my credit. This happens any time you take a loan. Companies want to make sure your credit is solid.

Applying for 10 cards signals trouble. Each "hard pull," or full application, decreases a person's overall credit score by about 10 points. My credit score would've been reduced by 100 points instantly.

Credit monitoring companies look for late payments and percentage of available credit being used. Using the cards to pay rent or payroll would've put me over the usual credit-to-debt ratio creditors recommend, dropping my score much more.

Creditors can tell if a person is struggling by their behavior. Frequent applications, debt transfers, or an erratic payment history is a sign of trouble. When borrowers do these things or come too close to maxing out lines of credit, they become high risk. Scores drop and rates increase.

If I'd said yes to this man, I'd have gone from highest ratings to high risk instantly. High risk people don't get zero percent offers. My rates would've risen to 21-35 percent, maybe higher. My debt would've compounded faster than the national deficit.

Game over. I lose.

Opening lines of credit to pay debt is called kiting. It's serious. If you're in this position, stop. Regroup. Cut your losses.

Just like planting that tree, the best time to manage debt is before it starts. The second-best time is now.

Saying yes to that offer would have made me bankrupt and homeless, and that man knew it. Luckily, I did, too.

There are three lessons in this story.

Lesson one: Opening a credit card is free. You should never have 10 cards, but if you do, close them slowly, starting with the worst first. Closing them too fast can hurt your credit score too.

Lesson two: Maintain one or two cards from good financial institutions. Use them responsibly. Don't go for shiny points over low interest rates unless you pay your cards to zero monthly, which is the goal.

Lesson three: There comes a time to say, "No more!" Make the tough decisions immediately. If there's a problem, be the first one on the phone to your creditors before they come looking for you. Communicate, then rebuild.

Avoid debt if possible. Read the fine print. If something seems too good to be true (Unsecured debt? Zero percent? No collateral?), it definitely is. Own your loans and chip away at them until they're gone.

There are two schools of thought on debt reduction. Some recommend starting with the highest interest rate debt first. Pay only the minimum on everything else and send every extra dime to the most expensive loan or card. When that's gone, dedicate that amount to the next highest interest rate debt, and so on until you're free.

Others like to pay off small debts first. The theory is you see the progress faster and you'll want to sprint to the finish line.

The mathematically correct way is to pay off the highest interest rate first. You'll save the most that way. I do something in between. I start with the most expensive debt, then see some low-hanging fruit and clear it off my desk. Whichever system you choose, be faithful. Post your progress somewhere visible. Celebrate victories. Be patient but consistent.

If you have a pile of debt, declare today the first day of rebuilding, and take one step every day. That's how you get to your final destination.

I'll see you there!

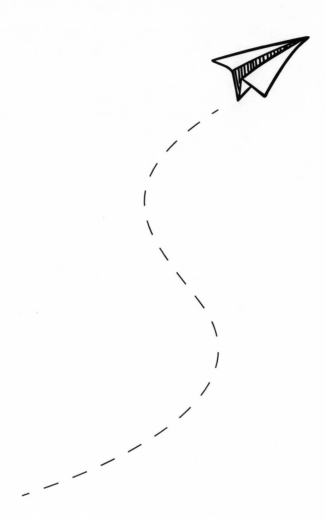

SECTION THREE
Be Rich

"Can anything be so elegant as to have few wants, and to serve them one's self?"
—Ralph Waldo Emerson

"I'd like to live as a poor man with lots of money."
—Pablo Picasso

"Wealth is the ability to fully experience life."
—Henry David Thoreau

Objective

Keep only things of highest quality—things, relationships, experiences.

Challenge the status quo and negotiate.

Realize this: You are gold. A diamond. A treasure.
Treat yourself that way.
Allow no less from others.

CHAPTER THIRTEEN
Typical Teacher Second Jobs

*"A dream doesn't become a reality through magic;
it takes sweat, determination, and hard work."*
—Colin Powell

It's hard to get a good job. Once, I applied for a job as a prostitute.

"Hostess," the ad said. I called the number.

"How old are you?" I was 19. Legal. The man started to schedule an interview until I asked a question.

"What are the hours and responsibilities?" I'd be carpooling with my dad whose bank was down the street.

"Responsibilities?" There was a long pause. "You get a private room with a shower. The client comes in…."

I'd worked in two restaurants and a fast food joint. None had a shower. I reread the ad. "Hostess—gentleman's club." This wasn't a country club where people ate after golfing. It was a *gentlemen's club.*

There wasn't one gentleman in that building.

Click.

Bartender. Waitress. Summer construction. Tutor. Those are typical teacher second jobs. Today, they don't have to be. I've worked on teams based all over the world, from San Francisco to New York, Chicago, and Panang. It felt like we were in the same room. Thanks to the internet, I collaborate with some of the best people in the world.

Anyone can make money remotely. One day, a student flashed his banking app. "Wanna see my passive income stream?" He made hundreds posting art on gaming sites. I've had students monetize YouTube channels, do street magic, grow family businesses, day trade, start a K-Pop dance studio, and turn lawn mowing into a landscaping business—all before graduation. If teens can do this, adults have no excuse.

"If I had your time...." people say.

You do. Your skills can make you money if you ask to be paid. You're in demand outside of school—if you decide to be.

Why You Need a Second Job

Second jobs are important for teachers, but not for the reason you might think. It's about staying marketable. Unless I stay in the "real world" I lose touch with it. It's easy to stagnate in teaching. Some people teach the same thing for 20 years. Blink, and the outside world has changed. I keep my skills sharp so I can shift on a dime if necessary.

This is critical today. Teaching is no longer the secure job it was a generation ago, one with lifetime benefits and guaranteed retirement. I can be teacher of the year and still be laid off while the district waits for numbers, projections, funds, or budgets. I've seen it happen.

"Don't worry," someone told a laid-off teacher. "You'll be fine. The money always comes in." To the one with the pink slip, that's no consolation.

"It takes a little bit out of me each time," said a teacher who's been laid off every year.

Imagine having four certifications and top ratings but

losing your job anyway, smiling for months knowing you'd be unemployed in June. That's what many teachers do.

In my time teaching, benefits have been slashed, retirements restructured, and every spring it's layoff season. Keeping current in other fields gives me confidence I can move on if necessary.

It also makes me a better teacher. When I say, "You'll use this in the real world to make money," students know it's true. They watch me do it. I promise never to teach something I don't use "for real."

Whether you're an administrator who's no longer teaching, a parent who stayed home to raise a child, or a career changer, if you've been out of a space for five years, you're obsolete. Keep up to date with skills. Develop new ones at any cost. Freelance, consult, teach a class, read journals, go to meetups, or join professional associations.

Before his passing, University of Rochester Vice President and Dean Paul Burgett was a high-level administrator who regularly taught a class in music or music history. This gave him incredible mileage as a leader. He knew how policies affected everyone from a first-year undergraduate to faculty and Ph.Ds. He remained relevant. His class was one of my favorites of all time.

"Today's graduate will have seven careers," I tell students. Not seven jobs, seven careers, according to the Bureau of Labor and Statistics. I thought they'd be shocked.

"That's a lot of opportunity," one kid said.

That's the mindset we need.

For a person my age, the job market feels like standing on quicksand. We're used to security. Students graduating today have never known a stable economy. They're used to constant change.

Embrace this perspective; it's a gift. Learn to view the

shifting sands as golden opportunities. Be confident, continually developing, and always in demand. Then use those skills to make more cash.

Sell Your Creativity

If you're the type of person who turns hairballs into holiday handbags, sell something. Start with things you love to make or do, or often do for free. Here's an example.

I make gemstone mala bracelets with little lotus dangles. I make them for me. The lotus is special to me: It's the flower that grows through the mud. It reminds me to grow in every situation—even the swampy ones.

Grow...through...the...mud. See...the...sun.

When people compliment the mala, I give them away. I make more. I give those away, too.

What if I sold them? I already know people want them. All I have to do is let them pay me, which they're happy to do, and I'm in business. This can be as simple as using a PayPal or Venmo address. Eventually it could become an online store.

You don't have to sell things. You can sell knowledge, too. Make courses. Organize or teach something fun. It doesn't have to be academic, just valuable.

If you like social media, become an authority on something and you'll have opportunities. The highest-paid YouTuber is a seven-year-old boy named Ryan who reviews toys. He's an authority. He'll never need another job.

Cute sells, but adults can do this, too. Jordan Page and Ingrid Macher built internet businesses out of their passions. Rhee Drummond, the Pioneer Woman, started her empire with a food blog.

Jordan Page is a Utah mother of six. She blogged and made videos about repaying debt while living on $35,000 a year. Jordan's content is about saving money, organizing, and raising a large family. She's like the friend I Skype when life gets out of hand.

Ingrid Macher wanted to lose 50 pounds. She did. She's now a "celebrity transformation coach" with 2.2 million Instagram followers. Ingrid pops up several times a day: "Hola, mis amores!"

"Buenos dias, bellezas!"

"Hermosa…."

She tells me to get up and exercise with her, sends a healthy lunch idea, or says something inspirational. I feel loved.

That's the secret to building a successful following. Bring value to a group but connect with the world.

Both Jordan and Ingrid have paid content, too. Jordan has courses and Ingrid has recipe plans sold in segments so you're never paying a whole lot for each one and you always want the next part. She now has a product line, too. She sells protein and oolong tea at premium prices. These things are dirt cheap at the store, but people pay Ingrid top dollar—because she's become a friend.

"Pioneer Woman" started out as a food and lifestyle blog. Rhee told stories about moving from LA to a ranch in Oklahoma while she cooked for her husband and the ranch hands. Now, everyone wants to eat and live like Rhee. Rhee's blog became a smash-hit show on the Food Network. She now has five cookbooks, a memoir, and a product line at Walmart. You know you've made it when your face is on the Mason jar display.

Each of these women started by talking about their passions. Eventually, they got paid. Then they kept the momentum going.

If you're tired of tutoring for pennies, look to things you love.

Start small. Ask, "Who would pay me for this?" Then, let them. That's what these women did. It works.

Be a Content Creator

I got my first tech job writing content. Start-ups need content.

"I see you have a blog," said Crystal, my first Silicon Valley marketing manager.

I didn't think my blog was a big deal, but it showed Crystal I was building an audience with zero training and that I could connect with people on several topics. That versatility has value.

I've written about business, finance, clean eating, education technology, reform, sustainability, science, martial arts, family life, fitness, food preservation, history, and health. These are things I know and love.

Study web writing and copywriting, then take some paying jobs. Education writing, "content writing," and "copywriting" are not the same. Content writing and copywriting are the things that makes you click—the opposite of the five-paragraph essay.

Do Teacher Stuff

There's always regular "teacher stuff" to do. Tutor, teach night school, write standardized test questions, or correct AP exams.

Today, instead of tutoring one student at the library, you can make a mini-class with five or 10 students using Google Hangouts and never leave your home. That's 10 paychecks collected in one time slot. That's how to grow your value.

You can also sell classroom materials you already have. My friend Alicia Sullivan has a TeachersPayTeachers store called

WriteSolutions. Alicia is building a nice side business using her existing teacher stash, redesigned for a larger market. If she wants, she could bundle it into a book and toss it on Amazon, too.

Work for an Edtech Start-up

Edtech start-ups need teachers. Most founders don't work in schools. You do. That's gold.

About five or six years ago, I took a call from a company with a platform I wanted to use, but they didn't have a mobile app.

"Sorry, I can't use this. My students use phones," I said.

"Go to the computer lab or get the laptop cart," the rep said.

I wanted to say, "Great idea! Thanks for the suggestion." At the time, we didn't have laptop carts, and there was one computer lab booked by the same guy every day. Short of challenging him to a duel for out-of-date computers, I wasn't getting access.

"No. We use phones." Even today not all schools have enough working computers, and most people default to their phones. Any multi-million-dollar company that doesn't recognize that is in trouble.

A year or two before that, I discovered another site for class. There was one problem: It required me to log in with Facebook. No teacher can log in with Facebook at school. I told the team. They listened and built an email login. Teachers used the site and it spread.

Most tech companies can't imagine the obstacles teachers face. You can get paid to make that connection. The smallest thing means the difference between viral use or slow death for a start-up spending $30,000 to $50,000 a month building their site. Your feedback saves time and money. It helps teams design products you'll use. It's like having a personal engineer.

Also, tech companies pay well.

Working in tech changed my view of what's possible in education. I watched brilliant people create world-changing things. Most people don't get to see that up close. I've been privileged to see it more than once. It's a powerful lesson. The impossible becomes possible when you take away the rules.

Getting Started

There are a couple of ways to jump into tech.

Find a hackathon like StartupWeekend or StartupWeekendEDU. These are competitions where teams assemble and build ideas into companies over a long weekend. You'll get an idea of how start-ups work and where you fit in.

You can also go to an edtech meetup or connect with companies online. Many have brand ambassadors and affiliates. You could end up with paid work.

If you're ready for full- or part-time work now, visit AngelList Jobs (http://angel.co/jobs) and EdSurge Jobs (https://www.edsurge.com/jobs).

AngelList started as a small email list curated by Silicon Valley entrepreneurs Naval Ravikant and Babak Nivi. It connected quality investors with companies who were fundraising. It's now a complete start-up ecosystem respected all over the world.

Angel List Jobs is free. It includes education companies but isn't limited to edtech. Nearly every start-up on the planet is there. Take a look and see what's available now or what trends interest you.

EdSurge is the leading edtech news source today. It was founded by Betsy Corcoran, formerly of Forbes, The Washington Post, and Scientific American. Betsy is an impressive human being building something big in education. EdSurge has articles and edtech data, does consulting for schools that want to better use technology, and has an education-specific jobs board that's free for teachers.

Here's a hint: Just because a listing says San Francisco, New York, or Boston doesn't mean you shouldn't inquire. Many people work remotely. Ask. You'll be surprised by what you find.

One Word of Caution

One word of caution: Some districts have rules you might not have considered before taking a side job in tech.

New York City fined teacher Jesse Owen $4,000 for creating his standards-based grading platform, Jumprope. He originally made it for his class, but people liked it and it spread. Eventually, Jesse quit teaching to build Jumprope, only to be dragged into court.

New York Public Schools had a 12-month "can't do that" clause. Jesse's fine seems steep, but the maximum could've been worse. Know your district's policy. Learn to recognize and avoid potential conflicts of interest between outside work and school. Keep the lines clear.

Another minefield to avoid: intellectual property arguments. If you do side work during school, the school may own the rights to it. Even if you use the school's Google Drive while at home you could be at risk. The law is unclear. Generally, the person with the best attorney wins. Intellectual property attorneys are expensive. Chances are you can't afford that fight, so don't have it.

Work honestly. Work on your time, with your equipment, and protect your intellectual property. Store master copies on your drive; it only takes two clicks for administrators to remove users from Google Drive. You could lose access at any time.

Keep up to date with policies, restrictions, non-compete clauses, and intellectual property law. Share freely but keep control of the material you worked hard to create. Then, consider using it to make some extra money in the spirit of "I'll just make more."

CHAPTER FOURTEEN
Time is Money

*"Making money is a hobby that will complement any
other hobbies you have, beautifully."*
—Scott Alexander

"Do nothing that has no use."
—Miyamoto Musashi

Before I could make money, I had to make time. I was
completely overbooked with obligations. I needed to return to the
question, "Does this get me closer to where I want to go?" Usually
the answer was no.

I learned a magic sentence: "I'd be happy to help. Here are my
rates."

When I said that, something amazing happened. I discovered
most people were willing to pay me. Some weren't, but they were
taking advantage of me. I left them behind. Removing things of
no value in *all* areas—spending, relationships, and time—makes
room for things and people that are of value.

It's not all about money. It is about valuing myself. When I do,
I say yes to things that matter.

Avoid These Common Mistakes

When I first tried to "just make more," I made mistakes. I said
yes to every freelancing opportunity. I didn't set rates. I took what

clients gave me and said, "Thanks." This is wrong. It's what I did when I babysat in high school: Parents gave me money at the end of the night and I said thanks. I didn't even count it until I got home.

Successful professionals don't do this. They set rates and bill for their time.

I was mentally stuck somewhere between "expensive teacher mode" and "dirt-cheap consultant mode."

The teacher in me overdelivered but was terrified to ask for money. More than once a simple job morphed into something much larger, yet I took the amount for the original job. Sometimes, people didn't pay me at all. If I had to ask a second time, I often let it go.

Because I was working so cheaply, people didn't respect me or my time. They'd send materials late or blow off meetings at the last minute because they "were busy." I wasted days waiting around. Sometimes they'd change the whole scope of a project after I was done so I'd have to redo the entire thing.

"You're underpricing yourself. I pay my graduate students more than that just to make a table of contents," said a professor-consultant I know.

Another friend said the same thing. "Double your rates," he said. "Triple, maybe. You work fast."

I started to set rates, but I made another mistake. I'd ask, "What's your budget?" This is wrong because people's budgets are always low.

Finally, I learned that magic sentence: "I'd be happy to help. Here are my rates." Simple. Matter of fact. No guilt. If a job mushroomed, I'd say, "I'd love to do that for you, too. Here are the rates." Before, I did the extra work for free.

If people missed calls and meetings, I didn't wait for them. I billed for the time. I raised my rates and stopped apologizing for charging. I was worth every dime.

When a waiter serves a Michelin-star meal he doesn't say, "Sorry, this is really expensive, but the chef's great, I promise." He presents the meal like an Oscar and says, "Please enjoy."

"I'd be happy to help. Here are my rates."

Before anyone else could value me, I had to value myself.

Often, that means learning to walk away.

The Lunch That Never Was

One day, I met an old friend for lunch. "Let's catch up," he said. We'd had catch-up plans before but when I arrived, he always had something else going on—work, a talk, a dinner, a workshop, a recruiting session. I'd take a back seat to his work, then go home. We never caught up.

I justified his behavior. "He's busy. He's important. He's got a lot going on."

This time, just as we sat, his phone rang. He excused himself "for a minute while I take a call." He left me with his assistant and a pile of papers. "Could you take a look at this?" He never returned from the call.

"This" was the workbook for an elite executive retreat. It needed an edit. By the end of my afternoon with the assistant, I'd effectively done a consulting job for free, yet his clients were paying him thousands to attend.

A year later, I said yes to coffee. He did the usual four-phone-call thing while I sat around. Between calls he had me look at a company he was working on. I'd been in tech for a few years by this point, so I was qualified to assess it. It was a series of high-end executive courses. It was excellent.

He said he needed someone who could handle public speaking to use the material in corporate settings and universities. It seemed like a good part-time opportunity, but I was maxed out. I was teaching during the day and had two tech jobs I loved outside of school.

The material was a perfect fit for my husband. He's passionate about personal development, coaching, team building, and efficiency. This was an area he knew and could promote. He's helped numerous small businesses grow, fixed broken teams, worked with everyone from military and law enforcement to executives on leadership and small business development, saved a factory more than a million dollars in process improvements, and onboarded millions of dollars' worth of franchisees to a company that's now a household name.

I told my friend I'd connect the two of them, but first, I discussed our financial situation. We were rebuilding. Buying, investing in, or joining anything was out of the question. We'd only be interested in contract or part-time work. He said he understood, and I made the introduction.

My husband went, but eventually he discovered it wasn't a job. He wasn't being hired to market, promote, and onboard people or grow the company. It was a high-emotion sales pitch: He could buy the courses and become an authorized speaker who could then sell to others for a commission. It was multi-level marketing. He'd been suspicious all along, but said, "No, that's not it." I hadn't seen it coming because I'd been honest with my friend.

When I learned the details and price, I was furious.

"He said we can make payments."

That was the moment everything clicked.

I was being treated poorly—in this situation and in many

others. Now it was affecting people around me.

Up until this moment, I allowed it.

At that moment I decided, *no more.*

Today, I would have handled every one of these interactions differently. For the "phone-call-leave-me-with-the-assistant," I would've said, "Looks like lunch won't work today. We can reschedule." Then I'd have left to enjoy my afternoon.

For the "can-you-take-a-look-at-this" editing job, I would've said this: "I'm happy to block off an afternoon to work with your team. Here are my rates."

I never would have had the phone-coffee-business disappointment because I wouldn't have taken that meeting. I would have recognized it as part of a larger pattern and declined.

"Fool me once," Abraham Lincoln said.

Guard Your Time

Time is precious.

It took time to learn to set clear guidelines for where "friend help" stops and work begins. I now volunteer selectively. It's the law of supply and demand. If I'm free and available—excessive supply—I'm cheap and taken for granted. If I protect my time, it has value.

I'm a fixer and helper by nature. I developed safeguards to avoid overcommitment.

I never say yes on the spot. I say, "I'll check my schedule" or "I'll get back to you." Often, I just say no. "I don't have the bandwidth for that right now."

When I do help, I do it in chunks and stages. I helped a friend with her website. She had excellent products but the site needed work. I made a checklist of tasks.

She didn't do the work. I stopped helping.

People see that I worked in tech or wrote a book. "I wish I could do that," they say. I'm happy to help—grateful to pay it forward—but most people have an excuse once I do something for them.

"Maybe when the kids grow up."

"I'm so busy now."

Those excuses don't sit well with me. When I was writing my first book, I wrote at four in the morning, left for school at 6:30, then came home from school and worked a second job. I worked hard.

When people don't do their part, I step away.

Karla, from the crowdfunding chapter, gave me advice I treasure: "Never do more than one labor of love at a time." She gives, volunteers, donates, and helps, but doesn't give to excess. She gives selectively. For the rest, she charges—at a premium—and people respect her.

Adam Rifkin, a Silicon Valley entrepreneur, is famous for the "five-minute favor." If he can do something for someone in five minutes or less, he goes out of his way to help. He can do a lot of good in five minutes, but he doesn't overburden himself.

I started working in tech because my friend Kamal opened doors for me. "There's a lot going on in edtech. I'd be happy to introduce you. Please feel free to take me up on that." That turned into my first Silicon Valley tech job.

Years later, he said what made me special is that I walked through those open doors—and most people didn't.

I could see this as I started to try to help others in return. I noticed I wasn't opening doors for people, I was also carrying them up 20 flights of stairs.

That's teacher behavior. I learned to stop.

Time is gold. Don't give your gold away like it's aluminum foil. Say yes selectively. Say no to make room for yes. Be the right kind of giver. Guard your time. Limited availability plus high expertise—that's why my friend gets to charge "those rates."

You can, too.

CHAPTER FIFTEEN
Eat Like a Chef for Pennies

"You don't have to cook fancy or complicated masterpieces—just good food from fresh ingredients."
—Julia Child

Eleven dollars and a grocery list. *"God, can I please have a sale…."*

Nobody respects the food budget. It always comes last. It's the water boy of the football team. Rent and mortgage are the all-star players. Car payments, utilities, and credit cards are the varsity team. Groceries don't even make JV.

During college, I lived off campus. Any cash left over was for groceries.

I had a food strategy. I ate at the diner where I worked. Then, a couple times a week, I went to the university's $2.35 all-you-can-eat breakfast and stashed enough fruit and cereal in my backpack to last days. It wasn't stealing. The football team ate more during breakfast than I packed.

At least I wasn't eating government cheese.

"You haven't lived until you've eaten government cheese," I told students. I don't think they issue "government cheese" to the needy anymore. It's poverty's neon-gold trophy, not quite dairy but classified as such, better suited to being a doorstop than food. We got it along with giant jars of USDA peanut butter that had more oil in it than an Exxon spill. Someone forgot to stir it once before taking a bite—that's how superglue was invented.

I don't wish government cheese or peanut butter anyone. Half a generation after government cheese, I still have flashbacks.

Food is one of the easiest places to save while you're rebuilding. You can feel like a millionaire and still get ahead. With a few shopping strategies and a little culinary skill, you'll eat like you've hired Oprah Winfrey's chef—all without a single coupon. Learn to cook from scratch, plan, and avoid waste. You'll cut your food bill in half.

Put the extra money toward your debt or dreams.

If you shop without a list, make multiple trips to the store, shop hungry, buy on impulse, or buy ready-made food, you're overspending.

Cook at home with fresh ingredients, in season. It'll do your spirit—and your budget—worlds of good.

"I can't cook," people say. Or, "I don't have time."

You can cook. And you do have time. I've always had multiple jobs, a family, and a life. Cooking and meal planning are all about strategy and a little bit of technique.

"Once you have mastered a technique, you barely have to look at the recipe again," said Julia Child.

I once burned tea while making kombucha, and somewhere out there is a pan with the outline of a grilled cheese sandwich because I was distracted by reading a book. Now, I'm proud of my cooking and I save a ton.

Here's an example: Hollandaise sauce costs six dollars for a tiny jar in the store. The ingredients are lemon, butter, and an egg yolk. I can make it for less than a quarter. Store-bought hummus is the same. A bag of chickpeas is $1.50. It makes enough to feed the entire nation on Super Bowl Sunday.

"If I had your time," one colleague said, looking at my homemade bread and apple butter.

You do have my time, I promise.

I mix dough at night and bake bread in the morning. I preserve, ferment, dehydrate, and can in season. A few hours of work equals a year of that food—jams, salsas, sauces, soups.

Overall, it takes me less time to make food than it does for my frozen-food friends to drive to the store and buy their boxes.

Food is important. We've become dangerously disconnected. Quality food doesn't grow in the grocery store. That's where food goes to die. America calls it "convenience food." I call it torture: three layers of packaging holding food hostage.

Preservatives. Shelf stabilizers. Colors. Texturizers. Guar gum. I don't even know what guar gum is.

There's an entire wall of dried, overpriced, pre-chopped veggies at the store. Mother Nature wraps onions so stores don't have to. Did you know baby carrots are just regular carrots shaved to fool you? They're not special. They shouldn't cost double.

Once we strip away shipping, packaging, "slot fees" (fees that stores charge to feature an item), and advertising costs, you see the real price of groceries. You'll be shocked at the extra you spend.

"Convenience foods" are relatively recent innovations. Prior to grocery stores, families lived off the land or went to dry goods stores where clerks filled their orders. Piggly Wiggly founder Clarence Saunders realized he could save on labor if people got their own cans and bags off the shelf, and in 1916 the "self-serve store" was born.

The grocery store as we know it developed in the 1950s and 1960s as strip malls invaded suburbia. Larger aisles, parking spaces, refrigerated cases, and shelf-stable food meant housewives could stock up on boxes and cans once a week instead of marketing daily. Everything was in one store.

"Dinner is served!" shouted as husbands walked in the door. "Just add water and heat!"

Liberation!

One of the meals I loved most as a kid was the TV dinner. Not only could we watch TV while we ate—strictly forbidden otherwise—we could choose our own processed meal. Other than TV dinner night, we ate what Mom made. On TV dinner night, I ate dessert first. "Dessert" was a tiny, congealed apple pastry lump in the top-right corner of a plastic tray that holds up the landfill three decades later. I was thrilled to be in control of my food for the first time in my life.

Most people my age grew up with cans and boxes. They were a status symbol, not a sign of poverty. Modern, prepackaged food. We were the first generation that didn't produce a large portion of our food fresh like our grandparents. Because of this, we're losing our food appreciation and skills.

Luckily, the farm-to-table, sustainability, clean eating, urban gardening, and artisan food movements are making food fashionable again. It's bringing all the foodie extremists together again—foodies and chefs, the health and budget conscious, environmentalists and locavores. Food production and preservation aren't just for great-grandmothers anymore. People used to laugh at me. Now, they ask me to teach them to can, garden, freeze, and dehydrate.

Just like my obsession with couponing, my food and homesteading passions started with fear. I was broke, so I decided I'd live off my land. If the pioneers could, so would

I. I read every book on urban gardening and watched all the YouTubers claiming to feed themselves. I learned this: It's hard. If I were a pioneer, I'd be dead.

I didn't save. I overspent on raised beds and garden structures. Two cheap greenhouses blew over in storms. City squirrels took a single bite out of every vegetable I grew.

Urban squirrels are no joke. They ate the side of my house. One carried a peanut butter jar from the recycling bin into a tree, then dropped it on the elderly neighbor's head while he worked on his car. That's a true story.

Done wrong, hobby homesteading is very, very expensive. It's why industrial farms exist.

In his book "The $64 Tomato," author William Alexander calculated the cost of each tomato he grew to be $64 after factoring in expenses. Still, I was inspired by stories like Barbara Kingsolver's "Animal, Vegetable, Miracle," and the Dervais family of Oakland, California, who live completely off their 8,000-square-foot yard. I had 10,000 square feet.

But you're not in Oakland.

Doesn't matter. I doubled down on kale, snuck veggies into flower beds, and designed a plan to replace the lawn with corn. People frown at drug addicts, but nobody says a thing when a person plants too much corn.

"Don't you have enough raised beds?" my husband asked.

"Nope." Every time he left for work, I'd install one more.

Luckily for the neighbors, we moved to the countryside before The Great Corn Project got underway. But moving only made my planting worse. In the country, farming is expected. Nobody bats an eye.

The more I planted, the more I killed.

I was about to admit defeat, then I noticed something. The

food I grew, foraged for, cooked, and preserved tasted better than store food. I felt healthier. I loved walking outside to find my dinner. There was always something delicious, even if I'd killed the exact thing I wanted. Nature usually gives us a Plan B.

Over time, I learned to garden and preserve. I stopped wasting my food because I appreciated how hard it was to produce. It tastes amazing. I can never go back to pre-packaged foods and chain restaurants again.

What began as a frugal food obsession turned into my "poser homestead." It's no longer insanity. It's a balanced, healthy lifestyle with some five-star food. Good food doesn't have to be expensive or difficult. The best food is simple, clean, and fresh, as Mother Nature intended. Learn to source ingredients, cook, and eat well. It's the best gift you can give yourself. Here are some suggestions to help save a ton on food while avoiding waste.

Meal Plan

Plan and prep meals for the week. Make a list, obey it, and shop once for ingredients, then stay out of the store. It's nearly impossible to go into a store for one thing—you'll buy 20.

I plan my meals with ingredients I find on sale and things I have at home that need to be used. I always look for value or seasonal ingredients, then plan the meals, never the other way around.

Once I have the staples and the sale scores, I raid the cabinets and Iron Chef up some amazing meals. When possible, I prep it all on the weekends or when I'm in a chef mood. Otherwise, I make a little calendar so I know what dinner is up next during the busy part of the week.

Shop the Source

Many foods are expensive in grocery stores but affordable at ethnic markets. I'm a regular at the Hispanic, Indian, Chinese, Korean, and Middle Eastern markets. It's like taking a trip around the world without a plane ticket, and ingredients are a fraction of the cost of the "international aisle" in the big supermarket.

Sometimes I mess up because labels aren't in English. Once I bought squid candy. I didn't eat it. Generally, my "mistakes" become opportunities. I find new ingredients I love.

Get a Pressure Cooker

My friend showed me her "bean pot"—a pressure cooker. My mom used one once. Her beef stew got stuck inside and is still at the dump. Today, I can't live without a pressure cooker. I learned to make dried beans in 20 minutes flat—a culinary miracle. No other piece of kitchen equipment does this so efficiently.

A good pressure cooker is an investment. Get a stainless steel one big enough to hold a nice pot of soup. Eight quarts minimum. Don't shortcut this. A pressure cooker pays for itself many times over with the time, fuel, and gas it saves. I can turn low-quality cuts of meat into restaurant-level meals. Things that usually take hours take 20 minutes.

The pressure cooker is having a well-deserved renaissance as the "Instant Pot." Every Amazon Prime Day and Black Friday they're on sale. Learn pressure cooking. Thank me later.

One thing to note: a pressure *canner* is not the same as a pressure *cooker*. Do not use them interchangeably. Ever.

"Recycled Food"

Soups and stews used to be poor man's food, but they're making a comeback. A well-crafted soup or bone broth is a meal unto itself. It's the mark of a good chef. Soup saves money. If I have food about to go bad, I make soup. I call it "recycled food."

"Cream of Mushroom" is really "Cream of Mushrooms That Would Have Rotted by Tomorrow Soup." I make a nice "Miso and Get Rid of That Zucchini Soup." Then there's "About-to-spoil Beef (and Barley) Soup."

I use the same concept to make casseroles, frittatas, pizzas, and salads. I turn wilting food into featured menu items.

If "recycled food" sounds unappetizing, translate your dinner into French and charge 20 bucks a plate. Garnish and serve. Guests never suspect a thing.

Cook in Bulk

I'm a force multiplier in the kitchen. I cook and freeze weeks of food at once. Instead of roasting one chicken, I cooked five yesterday—three plain, one tandoori, and another barbecue. It took exactly the same amount of time and made about 15-20 more meals.

Here's the process: First, roast the chickens. Cool them away from the dog that ate the Christmas ham. Cut the wings, thighs, and breasts off. Freeze in meal-sized food-saver bags. Pick off the remaining chicken and freeze for quesadillas and casserole. Finally, simmer some onions and celery and make a giant pot of broth from the bones. Freeze or pressure can it for soups, risotto, and stews. Get the chicken on sale (it was about $3.50 a chicken) and you've got some serious savings. If I can do this—and I'm a vegetarian—you can, too.

Don't worry; there's food for me, too. I made a rice cooker full of oatmeal and put it in five Mason jars—one for each work day. I boiled up a dozen eggs for snacks and made a week's worth of Weck jar salads. I also baked cookies, chopped veggie sticks, and made hummus for the week.

Done!

If you learn to can, freeze, and dehydrate, your bulk cooking could last you the year.

Here's the best part: I cook when I'm in the mood so that I'm inspired. It feels like art, not a chore.

There's always a strategy to my cooking. I want to eat like a gourmet, save money, and save time—in that order.

Keep it Simple

Simple, inexpensive ingredients make the best meals. Great chefs don't complicate things.

Another mark of a good chef is the ability to cook an egg. An *egg*. I didn't believe this until I studied Chef Gordon Ramsey's scrambled egg technique. Now I understand. Breakfast will never be the same.

This is the magic of simple ingredients. The things we overlook—eggs, beans, salads, fresh veggies—are gifts. They're brilliant foods, a canvas for the imagination, and nearly free.

Start small. Master one recipe or style at a time. Expand your repertoire. You'll never go back to frozen lunches again. Your wallet will thank you, but your palate and health will thank you more.

CHAPTER SIXTEEN
Hanging with Your Rich Friends

"The greatest discovery of all time is that a person can change his future by merely changing his attitude."
—Oprah Winfrey

I felt like I was on house arrest. I was saving money but losing friends.

"Let's go out to eat."

"Can't." I couldn't afford it, so I'd come up with an excuse.

What would a successful person do in this situation? I didn't want to be Broke Teacher anymore, but my wallet didn't agree.

How would Country Club Guy respond to this invitation, I wondered. Country Club Guy would go out with his friends.

Think of what you'll do instead.

Once, I made a broke teacher joke. The other person said, "Hey, you *wanted* to be a teacher!"

Everything about his tone said, "You made your bed; lie in it. *"You chose that career. You deserve whatever ramen life sends.*

At first I was annoyed at the comment. Then I realized something: I was annoyed at myself.

By scrounging, justifying, and playing the broke character on center stage, I made it real. Good actors become the characters they play. It was time to write a new script. It was time to stop reusing dental floss, to stop saying no and get back out on the town. I had to create a new definition of myself, a new self-image from the bottom up. I'd been scrounging so long I couldn't even afford dreams.

It was time to start living again. I'd start by reconnecting with old friends.

I still had less money than most of them, but I started asking "how can I?" instead of making an excuse for "why I can't."

With a few hacks, I could.

Surviving Restaurants with Not-Broke Friends

Going out to eat is the most terrifying thing during financial rebuilding. It's something people tend to suggest often and everyone takes it for granted. It adds up.

In my twenties, I had a crowd of friends who racked up huge bills on appetizers, drinks, steak dinners, and desserts. I'm a non-drinking vegetarian. Their bills were easily triple mine every time, so I developed battle tactics for dealing with restaurants.

First, I'd do the inviting. That way, I could control the setting and time. Lunch is always less expensive than dinner. That cuts the bill in half. For dinners, I'd look for good restaurants with discount days. If Tuesday is two-for-one night, you can bet I'm free on Tuesday. No one suspected I was being cheap.

If there were no discount days, I'd suggest a local diner or dive—a cult classic. No shame in that; it's shabby chic.

When someone else made the plans, I'd ask the server for a separate check. I'd pay my bill and tip well. If the server slapped down a group check, I didn't panic even though the total was more than my car payment. I picked it up first and left enough for my meal, including a generous tip.

When the "divide by seven" group math was off, I said, "Mine was 20 bucks. I left 30." I always over-tipped. They'd subtract my

30 bucks and divide the remainder.

For this to work, I had to carry cash in small bills. If I pulled out a card, this backfired. I ended up paying the whole bill with everyone thanking me for my generosity.

These days, there are apps that split bills. Everyone can pay for their meals without touching their wallet.

If eating out was still over budget, I'd invite friends over for a stock-the-bar party, pot luck, appetizer night, movie, or activity, or I'd cook from scratch. Fun by any means necessary.

A bad financial state should be temporary. Friends are forever. Keep good friends close. This is the biggest part of building a successful life.

Traveling in Luxury

It's not only restaurants that are tough while rebuilding. Traveling gets expensive, too.

One day, I went to Manhattan. "I'll crash on the couch," I told my friend.

"Get a nice hotel," he said. "Stop acting like a teacher and spend some money."

Nice hotels in Manhattan are no joke, but I found a great room dirt cheap using the HotelTonight app. I was upgraded to a jacuzzi suite. My luxury Manhattan hotel cost less than a normal dive. There are always deals if you know how to look.

HotelTonight books unsold rooms, Hopper uses piles of travel data to predict when you should buy airline tickets, and I learned the commuter rail is 25 percent less when taken during off-peak hours.

I save on travel by being flexible, booking with airlines directly, buying tickets in advance, traveling at uncommon times, or booking on Tuesdays—after the Monday sales cycle is released. I use commuter lots and trains rather than passenger trains when possible, and I travel light to avoid luggage fees.

Even when I'm booking with a sale site, I'll call the airline or hotel directly and ask if there's anything better. Sometimes there is. There are a few airlines that don't use booking sites, so I give them a call too.

When I arrive at my destination, I behave like a local, not a tourist. I save a ton and can enjoy higher-quality things.

There's something to this living well thing. The irony is this: Even living better, I spend much less overall because I'm not wasting and because I no longer spend my paycheck on my job.

That gives me the ability to do much more in the end.

CHAPTER SEVENTEEN
Runway Fashion at Big Box Prices

"The difference between style and fashion is quality."
—Giorgio Armani

"May I help you?" asked the saleswoman. I was panicking.

"Yes." I said. "I ate too much. I need to replace my entire wardrobe."

I hate shopping. I buy one comfortable thing in several colors, then stay out of stores for a decade.

I wasn't due to shop for five more years, then tragedy struck. I gained at least one pants size and was on my way to the next. At first I was in denial, then I stepped on the scale.

I tried to fit into my clothes, but whalebone corsets are hard to find outside of Victorian England, so I subscribed to my favorite store's list and I waited for the "We haven't seen you in five years" coupon. I bought two pairs—one size up—then unsubscribed.

Life was good until I remembered school was right around the corner. I needed new work clothes, too. Each button was an inch from its buttonhole.

My nine-year-old offered helpful advice. "Hey Mom," he said, "you should get some pants that are friends with your thighs."

Others were kinder.

"You look really good," said my metro fashion friend. "You

gained weight. You don't look like you came out of the camps anymore. Don't change a thing." That compliment didn't make my pants fit, though.

I had to act fast, but I didn't have a lot to spend.

Investing in school clothes is pointless. School destroys clothes. It wrecks Dior before it walks in the door. Kid sludge is everywhere. Little kids pick their noses, then tug on dry-clean-only favorites. It's no safer for high school teachers. Coffee and salad dressing fly through the air as teachers sneak lunch at their desks.

"We need a uniform," I said. Something simple: golf shirts and khakis. Textbook business casual. I'd buy fewer clothes and wouldn't cry when they got wrecked. Kids could spend their money on phones instead of overpriced, pre-ripped hoodies.

No one liked my idea, so I made a uniform myself. It was corporate "business casual"—neat and cheap. The suit was dying a slow, painful death anyway, reserved for Wall Street commuters in hangman-noose ties sleeping their way to meetings on the Thursday morning train.

"Is it *dress-down* day?" A colleague questioned my khakis.

Dress-down day is a sacred privilege we pay for. If we do, we can wear jeans on Fridays. In my corporate life, Friday jeans were free—an early start to the weekend.

Paying to wear jeans was silly. If someone could see me in jeans on Friday, why not Monday? My nice jeans, boots, and suit jacket were more professional than Buttcrack Dude's 20-year-old stained, ripped Dickies that were "weekday approved." Charging us to fund clubs that the school should have paid for anyway? That was extortion.

People should dress neatly, but whether it's jeans, khakis, or a dress shouldn't matter.

In tech, everyone wears jeans, T-shirts, and hoodies. I wore a suit to my first tech event. Mistake. "Go get a hoodie," my friend Heather said.

I didn't have any hoodies, so a co-worker sent me three. I was ready to take on the tech world.

Not everyone in tech wore a hoodie, though. Some wore jeans, T-shirts, boots, and nice blazers. It was "the Silicon Valley suit." My friend conducted big deals in a John Varvatos designer T-shirt and dark, boutique jeans. I never heard anyone ask him if he paid for dress-down day.

I got to thinking: If the smartest people I knew built multi-million-dollar companies wearing jeans, I could dress comfortably. Research says people feel less intimidated when they aren't faced with The Suit. It leads to better relationships and better results.

Of course, there are also convincing studies showing dressing up makes us feel powerful and confident, which may raise job performance. As any big-data-era educator knows, when presented with conflicting data, always pick the data that supports your point of view. I kept my khakis. I wore that "uniform" for several years.

One day, I no longer wanted to. I felt boring and I wanted to dress better.

I discovered a few fashion secrets that helped me venture into the world of better style.

Ways to Save on Clothes

I study sizing; each designer is a little different. If I know my exact sizes for each designer, I can shop online and get giant discounts. Staying out of the store means I don't buy extra, and it saves time.

When I needed to replace my wardrobe, I found my favorite clothes cheap, one size up, at Poshmark and ThredUp. Poshmark is an app and website. It's like eBay for clothes. People shop from each other's "closets." Sellers get credit for sales they can use or cash out.

ThredUp is designer thrift. People send in designer clothes in postage-paid bags. ThredUp credits sellers for items they accept and donates things that aren't in acceptable condition. Shoppers shop from the inventory. I have upper-end clothes from both sites and I've sold on Poshmark, too. It's easy and fun.

Now, I can eat bagels all day without living in fear of my pants.

Consignment stores have good clothes, too, especially now that minimalism is growing in popularity. I got my high school prom dress at the Salvation Army for 19 dollars. "#GIRLBOSS" author Sophia Amoruso built an empire picking through thrift stores and featuring "vintage" (translate: used and washed) items on eBay. It's not all junk; there are upper-end consignment stores and vintage boutiques.

I'm brand sensitive. I sign up for brand emails, then buy what I need, then unsubscribe to avoid email overload. This is my one exception to "no coupons" because I'm getting a specific thing I need and I know they'll send me a 40-percent-off email. I'm not tempted to impulse shop.

I compound these savings by shopping "end of season." That's when prices are lowest. It's really not "end of season." It's more like "two weeks into the season." Retailers swap out fashion so far in advance that there's plenty of time to wear everything before the weather changes.

If I'm in the store, I ask for additional discounts. Often, there are.

"Would you like to sign up for our store credit card? You'll get an additional 25 percent off today." That one I refuse. These are high-interest cards that cause a hard-pull on credit. I don't need bad store cards weighing me down.

Deep discount sites like 6pm.com are also blessings if I'm looking for something specific and don't want to be tempted to buy more. They're deeply discounted. If you're an impulse shopper, though, stay away. "Only one left in your size!" will get you every time.

One trick I like to use while shopping online: I abandon my cart. I click on everything I want, then click out of the site. Because sites can trace users, a day or two later, I often get an email that says, "Did you forget something?" That's invariably followed by a coupon.

There are also Google Chrome extensions that automatically look for coupon codes.

If I stick to my list *and* get a bigger discount, I win.

If you love expensive fashion but don't wear it often, there are companies like Rent the Runway that let you rent designer items and return them like library books once your supermodel pictures are plastered all over social media. Or you can keep buying and reselling clothes on Poshmark. You can buy and sell upper-end purses on Rebag.com. "Clothing arbitrage" is now a legitimate side or full-time job. People hunt for underpriced designer items on sale and sell them at higher, but still discounted, prices.

How to Calculate Value

It's not the cost of an item that determines the value, it's the "price per wear."

PRICE ÷ NUMBER OF WEARS = PRICE PER WEAR

The lower the price per wear, the better the value. Wearing an expensive item constantly for a couple years is much better than leaving something you got on sale in the closet.

I have an expensive dress I wore a few times. If someone asked, "Want to pay 75 dollars every time you wear this dress?" I'd have come to my senses. Meanwhile, I have quality boots and shoes I wear constantly. On the surface, they appeared outrageously expensive, except I wear them all the time and I love them. That's a far better value than the unworn dress or sale clothes sitting in the drawer.

Don't shop sales, shop value. If you get value on sale, even better.

Buy What You Need

I know a teacher who doesn't buy clothes—ever. She sews, hems, wears shoes into the ground, and debates whether she can afford a new bra. It's important to buy good things. Not buying quality undergarments is serious for a female. Doctors and chiropractors are way more expensive than clothes.

Although undergarments don't affect me, running shoes do. Runners swap out shoes every 500 miles. That's a pair or two a year for a serious athlete. One year I got shin splints.

"When was the last time you bought shoes?" my sister asked. She runs marathons. It had been three or four years since I'd bought a pair. I needed new ones. Injuries cost more than proper equipment.

Having the wrong gear can sometimes be a matter of life and death. My dad almost died climbing Mt. Washington in the winter.

It was his first winter climb and his base layer was too big. For winter mountaineering, the layer closest to the skin fits tight to evaporate sweat—if it feels a little too small, it's doing its job. If it's loose, like a regular shirt, sweat doesn't wick away, it freezes. In the middle of February, that's not merely a comfort issue. With a wind chill of a hundred below, it'll kill.

I'll wear decade-old shirts proudly, but when it comes to things that matter, I buy quality and I take care of it so it lasts. Cheat on health or safety items and you'll give that cash to the doctor or funeral director instead.

When I shop, I look for places with good customer service, free or fair-priced shipping, and easy returns.

Eddie Bauer had a manager, Daniel, who remembered me every year even though I only shopped at Christmas. He asked about my family and knew our tastes and approximate sizes.

Gerry at Hunt Photo noticed me researching high-end Nikons when I was switching from film to digital. He found me a professional-grade Nikon someone traded in, then helped consolidate all my cheaper lenses into two professional ones I really needed.

Jardin, the company that makes Foodsaver, resent my order because it went to my old address—a year after I moved. I'm certain it was my fault, not theirs. They also replaced a broken Foodsaver after nearly three years.

Compare that with a big-box retailer who wouldn't let me exchange duplicate baby shower items, clearly unopened, because I didn't have the right gift receipt.

Look for retailers who go the extra mile. Buy used if it makes sense. Shop wisely. Skip unnecessary purchases. Get things that will make you happy, but only when you need them. Stop the "I'll make do" cheap purchases and don't buy just because something's on sale. Buy intentionally and buy the highest quality you can.

Do these things and you can save the world from bad teacher clothes—affordably.

You'll feel like a million without spending one.

CHAPTER EIGHTEEN
How to Get the Best Teaching Job

*"If you can't see yourself working with someone for life, don't work
with them for a day."*
—Naval Ravikant

"My mom doesn't want me to be a teacher!" my student said.
"She said I'll be broke forever."

"You're throwing your life away!" My friends intervened when I
left corporate America to teach.

Would you be proud if your friend, child, or little cousin
wanted to teach? Or would you tell them to pick computer
science?

No one goes into teaching to be rich, but you can do well if
you pay attention to the job hunt. Most teachers do this all wrong.

"You'll never get a job! There's a million history teachers."
That's what everyone told me during grad school. After I was
hired, people said, "You're lucky to have a job." Neither message
set me up for success. Constant negative reinforcement put me
in desperation mode at job hunt time. If Principal Lucifer offered
me a job in Dante's Middle School, I'd have said yes without
hesitation.

How could I properly evaluate job offers or find opportunities
if I was programmed to think I was lucky to get an interview at
all? We're suffering a severe teacher shortage, yet I was dog-
trained to accept the first offer I received without question out of

fear.

By contrast, companies have bidding wars for engineers.

We're about to do three things to turn the tables on the typical teacher job hunt: research, negotiate, and ask key questions.

Job hunting is where good strategy pays off in spades.

Gatekeepers

When I first started job hunting I went to a large urban district in my region.

"Here's the application," said the woman at the central office desk. She didn't look up. It was an application for substitute teachers.

"I'm here to apply for this position, please." I tried to show her the paper. She still didn't look up.

"You've got to substitute."

"No, thank you. I was sent to apply for this job. I'm not applying to substitute."

When I walked in, she was mildly annoyed. Now, I'd made her angry. I finally had her attention and she was deeply committed to not helping me.

I asked one last time. "How...do I apply...for *this job*?"

Then I realized something.

If it was this much trouble to hand in a piece of paper, I wouldn't like working in this district. I left.

There was an elite boarding 45 minutes from where I grew up. It always intrigued me. Kings, princes, and actors sent their kids there. Maybe I'd take a quick peek. I put on a conservative suit and took a ride to the admissions building.

"I'd like to observe a class, please." I told the woman in

admissions of my interest, qualifications, childhood connection to the region, experience, and degrees, and that I might be interested in applying to join their community.

Private boarding schools charge a lot, but they don't pay well, and they overwork their staff, so they're generally in recruiting mode. One of my graduate professors was faculty in residence there at the beginning of his career. He said there were a lot of rules about visitors and activities, and that he worked or was on public display 24 hours a day.

"I don't think we can do that." She wasn't going to let me visit. She had a list of reasons. *It simply would not be possible.* She was quietly rude, pretentious, and condescending, yet the smile never left her face.

Like the woman at the central office front desk, she was the gatekeeper.

Education is filled with gatekeepers. Often, we don't recognize them, which is precisely why they're so difficult to get around. It's why many high-quality people don't apply to be teachers. One of the best teachers I know nearly changed careers because the teacher prep gatekeeper kept changing course requirements on his group midstream.

After a 10-year corporate career, I fought for certification over a "technology test" mis-scored by gatekeepers who didn't know technology.

Gatekeepers are everywhere. The nicer they seem, the more dangerous they are. In both situations, they lost a good candidate.

If something about a job feels off, your intuition is giving you a gift.

Work somewhere you love. Kids are kids everywhere. Look for adults with a philosophy that matches yours.

"If you can't see yourself working with someone for life, don't work with them for a day," said investor and entrepreneur Naval Ravikant. Naval can afford to say that: He's the co-founder of AngelList (as mentioned in Chapter 13). But it wasn't always that way for him, either. In the beginning of his career, he worked in difficult situations. Now, he has his own company.

You probably won't build your own school, but you can choose wisely.

"These people treat me terribly but I know this job will be *great!*" said no one ever. By the time you realize you're with toxic people—or even people who are good *but not good for you*—the damage is already done. Cut your losses as quickly as possible.

The Job Hunt

I got my first teaching job at a job fair with 10 decks of cards stacked against me. I co-owned a business, so I couldn't pack up and move. I looked young, so people judged me. I was living in a state where everyone knows everyone, and I wasn't related to a single person. And I went to the job fair on crutches.

"What do you teach?" a recruiter asked.

"Social studies." History teachers are a dime a dozen. Had I been math, science, or computer science, choirs of angels would've sung my praises while the room organized a single-elimination boxing tournament for my approval.

But social studies? Recruiters kicked my crutches to get to the math guy behind me.

I had a solid resumé and nearly a decade of corporate experience, but everyone told me to "jump at the first offer—you'll be lucky to get it." I ended up with two offers. I took the first, sight unseen, without hearing the second. It was a good job, but what if the other one was better? I'll never know.

Compare, negotiate, research, and ask the tough questions upfront. Let there be no question about the value you bring to the table.

I wish I'd known to research schools better, to ask about school culture, procedure, leadership, benefits, policy, opportunities for advancement, or to negotiate salary because of my decade of relevant industry experience. Other people got higher starting pay with similar or less experience. "You'll be lucky to get a job," was all I heard.

Do Your Research

Not all teaching jobs are created equal. You want the perfect job—for you. Research everything. Talk to people. Salary is important, but a million other things make or break the work day, such as district environment, ability to advance, condition of the school, and extracurricular activities.

First and foremost, make sure you can afford to take the job.

Average starting teacher pay in 2011 was $33,950 according to TeacherPortal.com. With one to four years' experience, teachers earned nearly $36,000. With five to nine years' experience, slightly more than $41,000. Top-step teachers averaged $56,000.

Is your potential district offering enough to cover your basics after deductions? That's your bottom line. Don't accept a job that pays less unless you're a two-income family or will get a second job to make up the difference. Be transparent about your needs.

"Unfortunately, those numbers don't work for me. What can we do?" Base salary for teachers is often cast in stone, but many districts pay for experience, degrees, certifications, or give opportunities to earn more for coaching or taking on extra duties. Asking "How can we make this work?" is the responsible thing to do. Show a commitment to your own value. This conversation could make the difference in being able to say yes to a lower-paying district you love.

Know the average pay for the region. "I notice the three districts around pay significantly more." Make a counteroffer. You might succeed.

Ask about benefits like retirement, medical contributions, union dues, and other things that will be deducted from your check. These are valuable benefits, but if they drop you below your minimum survival line, you're in trouble.

Some schools require teachers to coach or work outside the school day as part of the job. This could prevent you from taking a second job if that's part of your plan. All that information goes into your final decision.

Someone Will Research You

Before you research schools, research the most important thing—yourself.

I was researching a company for my second job. Google said the founder was an international con artist. Something seemed wrong, though. I'd been on the call with the guy. He sounded younger than the mug shots online. I dug deeper.

The criminal was a different person in the same field, originally from the same region, with an identical name and a few matching details.

Do you have the same name as an infamous con artist? Find out. Google yourself. If there's anything false or inaccurate, you want to find it first. "You might've noticed I have the same name as this international criminal…that's not me. I'm the author, teacher, and blogger." It may not land you the job, but at least your resumé won't be mysteriously tossed in the trash.

One day, I asked students a question: "Where would you go to find a picture of me at a party?"

It was the scavenger hunt of the century. Every kid wanted to be the one to find the blackmail picture.

They scoured social media and finally gave up. "Where's it at?" someone asked.

"Nowhere," I said. "It doesn't exist." My social media is grandmother safe. "When in doubt, leave it out," I say. It's never too late to improve your digital image. If yours is good, make be better—be better than the best.

My brother had a conversation with a Disney employee. "See this scene? Every blade of grass is individually drawn. Could we have gotten away with coloring it all green? Yes. But we don't. Because we're Disney, and that's what we do."

Because we're Disney, and that's what we do.

Disney's the best. Follow their lead.

Start with your professional profiles. Check and update them two or three times a year. I get connection requests all the time from people who don't even have a profile picture on their LinkedIn. Why would you want that to be my first impression of you? At best it gives the impression you don't pay attention to detail, and at worst that you're not up to speed with technology. Both could cost jobs.

I have a friend who doesn't use LinkedIn. He's an investor. They use AngelList. He keeps a skeleton profile on LinkedIn with a link driving people to AngelList and Amazon.

Profiles exist for people to find you. Keep yours current, in places where people look. Link people to places where they see you at your best.

Negotiate

A school found you. They love everything about you. You're about to get an offer. Now what?

In the business world, people negotiate. Interviews should be a conversation, not a firing squad.

Adam Galinsky is the chair of the management division at the Columbia Business School in New York City and the author of "Friend & Foe: When to Cooperate, When to Compete, and How to Succeed at Both." He's a negotiation expert. Galinsky says it's important to do your research and to feel invincible when negotiating.

I don't always feel invincible, so how do I pull that off?

Galinsky tells candidates to pause before a negotiation. Recall a time they felt powerful and confident, even if they don't at the moment. Resurrecting feelings of power and confidence helps in negotiation, and it's always a negotiation—even in education where everything's done by contract. Something has wiggle room, even if it isn't base salary.

Author and heavyweight boxer Ed Latimore wrote about this in "The Four Confidences." "In many cases, you don't have to experience success in a specific field to feel confident in your ability to thrive there. Rather, you can remember and rely on the confidence gained from past success in other disciplines to carry you."

Confident people negotiate with authority. In return, they're treated like experts, not part of the herd.

Go in strong. Know your plan B. That's critical. You can't judge an offer unless you know the next-best alternative.

In business, this is called the "best alternative to a negotiated agreement" or BATNA. Roger Fisher and William Ury coined this term in their bestseller "Getting to Yes: Negotiating Without Giving In." Knowing the next-best alternative enables you to decide whether the offer in front of you is good when compared with other possibilities.

Your next-best alternative may not be ideal. It might mean taking a job you don't really want for the experience. It might not even be a job offer. It could be keeping your barista job to stay available for something you really want.

Do you know what your next-best alternative is?

Do you have a counteroffer based on research?

More importantly, do you have a line in the sand beyond which you're prepared to say no? At what point will you walk away without remorse?

When you know the answers to these questions, you're ready to interview. Prepare for these conversations like a researcher. Go in with confidence. Then, you're invincible.

CHAPTER NINETEEN
Teacher Housing Projects?

"Home is heaven for beginners."
—Charles Henry Parkhurst

"If you never remember anything else I say, hear this," said Monica. "When you buy a house, you're going to want to kill people."

I figured the pain would range somewhere between a bad tax season and a day of cleaning moldy food out of the fridge. Monica sensed I wasn't taking her seriously.

"I mean it. You will literally want to kill people. Don't." Her face changed from Perfectly Nice Monica to one which reminded me of "America's Most Wanted." She'd bought a house. She knew.

The stress of moving is second only to the stress of the job search. Housing is your biggest expense; you need a place you'll enjoy. With a little research and planning, you can find one.

Teacher Housing Projects?

How about living in a housing project? Many communities are designing teacher subsidized housing to make teaching affordable in expensive parts of the United States. This seems thoughtful for places where housing is expensive or teacher pay is low, but I've spent my life trying to get kids out of projects, not show them careers where they'll go back in.

The San Francisco housing crisis is the most extreme example. According to a 2016 report by SmartAsset.com, you need a $216,129 salary to even think about renting a two-bedroom apartment. Teachers don't come close. Shacks in tear-down condition with no land are selling for over a million.

A two-bedroom apartment in New York City averages $3,692 a month, meaning your first $44,304 each year goes to rent. This year's starting salary for first-year teachers was $56,711. After rent, this leaves a thousand dollars a month for student loans, utilities, food, and transportation. Detroit, by contrast, is affordable. It's possible to rent and live well with a salary of $37,000 per year.

All this affects students. Great teachers choose districts they can afford. I've had Bay Area friends whose rent increased over a thousand dollars in one lease renewal. When this happens to teachers, they quit mid-year and leave the area. They can't move; there are bidding wars for apartments and houses.

Is "teacher housing" the right approach?

In districts I researched, inventory for housing programs was limited and pay guidelines disqualified most teachers. In Los Angeles, for example, teacher's aides and custodians qualified for assistance, but teachers were just a bit over the income line.

The town of Hertford County, North Carolina built three subsidized apartment buildings for teachers. North Carolina is one of the lowest-paying states for teachers, so housing was a key part of recruitment.

Some teachers don't want an apartment, they want to buy a home. The U.S. Department of Housing and Urban Development tried to help with the Teacher Next Door and Good Neighbor Next Door programs.

HUD allows teachers, firefighters, police, and EMTs to purchase homes in "renaissance locations" at steep discounts. A renaissance location is an area in transition. In plain English, these homes are in tough neighborhoods that need work.

We bought our first home in a HUD auction.

It belonged to a drug dealer who defaulted on his government loan. We swapped out the black lights, tore out rugs, painted over blood spatter, and dealt with a list of regulations longer than the Code of Hammurabi.

It was a lot of red tape, but we got a great starter home in a safe area.

The HUD Teacher Next Door program is a great idea, but not for everyone. Teachers have to buy in cities where they work, and there aren't always homes available. This gives our San Francisco friends zero chance of finding a home that qualifies, as there was no inventory there at the time of this writing.

To date, between 400 and 500 teachers have taken advantage of the Teacher Next Door program. With 3.2 million teachers, this doesn't put a dent in demand. If only half a percent need housing, HUD needs 16,000 qualified homes in the right places. Five hundred successes doesn't come close to matching demand.

Many of these programs are "I won the lottery" deals for people who can coordinate job and housing searches in areas with large HUD home inventories. I did a quick search. There were houses available in my state, but none in my district. I can't use this program.

Texas has a program called Texas Heroes. Public servants can apply for low fixed-rate mortgages to buy any home. Some also get down payment assistance ranging from two percent to 5.125 percent based on creditworthiness, and there's a $2,000 mortgage credit for first-time homebuyers.

New Jersey built teacher housing, too. Newark's Teacher Village bet that housing-starved Manhattan teachers would cross into New Jersey for a "like-minded community." Teacher Village features parks, daycares, and schools. I'd love this. My husband? Not so much. He'd rather be on a farm commune than a teacher one. Teachers, he says, can't talk about anything besides school. For this reason, I won't be in a place like Teacher Village anytime soon.

Tulsa, Oklahoma has been talking about housing as well. Oklahoma has affordable housing—it's nearly 30 percent cheaper than the national average—but Oklahoma's pay is among lowest in the nation for teachers. Texas and Arkansas routinely poach Oklahoma's border teachers because they pay so much more.

To partially address this, the OHFA4Teachers program grants loans to qualified Oklahoma teachers. Still, a teacher with a salary of $35,000 can't pull this off.

According to experts, you should spend 20 percent or less of your income on housing. Today, we spend much more. A January 2015 study by the Pew Charitable Trust showed housing takes up to 31 percent of income for the top fifth of Americans, and 40 percent for the bottom fifth. This means people with the least to spare spend the highest percentage of their wages on shelter.

Do your housing homework. Look for a good place within a reasonable commute zone, then negotiate everything you can to get the best deal possible.

Start with School

If you're moving to an area with a teacher shortage, ask if there's a moving allowance or benefits to help with the move.

Some districts use recruiters who have access to perks. Moving assistance is more common with corporations, so the answer may be no. If so, save your receipts. You may qualify for a tax deduction.

Research the Possibilities

My first mortgage was zero percent down, fixed rate, with a payment even a grad student could afford. Those were the days of easy credit. Even my dog was getting Visa applications. Getting a mortgage is harder now, and if you want to remain mobile, buying isn't an option. With fewer people buying, rent is on the rise in popular areas.

You don't need "popular." You want affordable, safe, a good commute, and a neighborhood that makes you smile. Look for hidden gems in up-and-coming areas, slightly off the beaten path. Learning to spot them will cut a big chunk off your housing bill.

I moved a lot in my twenties, so I got pretty efficient. I developed a system.

First, I researched apartments (and later houses). I made a short list of neighborhoods I liked. I researched, then talked to anyone who lived there. That cut down the list.

Next, I drove around several times—at night, during the day, and on a weekend. If I liked the feel, I'd come back. I'd go running, hang out in coffee shops, and talk to strangers on the street or in stores. I would've knocked on doors and windows if it weren't creepy. I wanted to know the area before I signed on the dotted line.

The first house we bought was a mile from the airport on a double lot of land on a dead-end street. It was safe but loud—a decent trade-off for a good commute at a price we could afford.

Earlier, I lived in a rundown apartment owned by a slumlord. It was two streets over from the rich neighborhood, but technically over the city line, which cut the rent in half. It was only a block from coffeehouses, restaurants, and the running trail.

The slumlord said I could paint and wallpaper. Later, I realized that wasn't kindness, it was a slumlord getting an inexperienced renter to rehab the place for free. When I left, she raised the rent from $325 to $875. Not a bad profit for someone who never did any upkeep.

"I collect rent on the first of the month," she said. She'd park her Mercedes and go knocking on doors with her bouncer-looking brother-in-law.

"I work. Where can I mail the check?"

She didn't want to give an address. She'd never had a tenant with a job. She was a textbook Section 8 landlord. When the second-floor lady kept bringing in cockroach-invested furniture from dumps and curbs and refusing to let non-white exterminators do their job, she didn't care. When the new second-floor husband beat his family routinely, she threatened to evict me for "costing her money" by calling the police. When the toilet kept breaking it took her months to call a plumber until I held my rent in escrow and threatened to invite the building inspector for lunch.

Over time, the neighborhood began to change. My car was broken into. The second-floor abuser started to threaten me. It became stressful coming home. It was time to leave.

Good housing is important.

If good housing is too expensive, look for roommates, upcoming areas, or unfilled housing complexes with deals like a month or two free. Independent landlords sometimes negotiate a discount for lawn mowing or groundskeeping, too.

Get creative but don't compromise on things like a good commute and safety. You want to look forward to coming home at night.

Consider Your Commute

A bad commute turns a dream job into a nightmare. Think of drive time, wear and tear on your car, parking fees, insurance, trains, subways, and busses before you move.

During grad school, I kept my corporate job on weekends. I worked two 10-hour days. My drive was two hours and 20 minutes each way. I didn't mind the drive. It was relaxing and my corporate salary and benefits were excellent. I had one serious issue, though: My car lease had a mileage limit.

I don't recommend leases, but I ruptured my left Achilles tendon at the beginning of student teaching. My car was a stick shift. I needed an automatic on one day's notice to student teach. I was a grad student with a new house—I couldn't get a car loan. Saturn offered me a leased automatic. I knew I'd blow away the mileage limit, but I said yes. At the end of the lease, God intervened. My dealer ran a special, asking for lease trade-ins and offering to waive mileage penalties for people buying a car.

Continually buying new cars is a terrible deal and something that puts many people behind in their finances. They end up owing more on the first car than the trade-in value, which dealers happily add to the new loan. That's how you stay in car debt forever. In this situation, though, I saved myself several thousand dollars in penalties and escaped with my life.

When I buy a new car, I get a good one, pay it off early, then drive it forever. I continue to make the car payments to my savings account with the idea of paying for the next car in cash.

The bottom line is this: You need a great place to live and a reliable way to get there. Then, you can put your energy where it belongs: in the classroom.

CHAPTER TWENTY
You Have to Pay Taxes...I Think

"The only thing you have to do is pay taxes and die."
—Unknown

My birthday is five days before Tax Day. I was born on Holy Saturday, but sometimes my birthday falls on Good Friday, a Catholic day of prayer and fasting.

"Your birthday isn't the center of the universe, you know," God said.

He sent a reminder when I got older. April 15th. Tax Day. Five days after my birthday. If I thought I could eat cake on Good Friday behind God's back, I couldn't outwit the IRS.

The IRS has been ruining my birthday ever since.

I loved "Refund Day" when I was younger. It was like winning the lottery. I know it's just me getting my own money back while the government earns the interest, but in my twenties it felt like a large chunk of cash.

As I got older, the refunds stopped. I started getting bills. I was freelancing, working several jobs, and for 11 months of the year, I made progress reducing debt and got ahead. But April defeated that illusion.

One year, I made enough money to pay off my student loans, but I didn't send it right away. I logged into the bank every day to look at it. I liked the feeling of seeing a pile of money in there. I'd never had so much. I wanted to withdraw it all in one-dollar bills. I'd stack it, fan it, toss it in the air, and make a rap video.

None of that happened, nor did I pay off my student loans.

I got an email from my accountant. "Here are your taxes."

It was the tax bill of the century. Because of a perfect storm with the business—which had enough to pay the employees but didn't pay us—we owed nearly $35,000 after my withholding was gone.

I drained my bank account and made a payment plan for the rest.

A month after I paid off the balance, April came again. It brought another large bill despite over-withholding.

This happened three years in a row.

But don't worry, this is the newer, friendlier IRS. They don't put people in debtor's prison anymore. As long as I made the payments, Uncle Sam smiled.

Still, owing the IRS isn't a place you want to be. There are fees, penalties, and interest. The rate looks low, but it isn't. It compounds by the Olympic stopwatch second.

If you're teaching, and that's your only job, and you withhold properly, you probably won't have an issue. But if you start making more money on the side—which is our goal here—you have to be ready.

I like to think of taxes as a video game. I shoot down my income with legitimate deductions and get as close to zero as possible. This is one of the few times in life where looking poor helps.

I recommend hiring an expert. Tax season is no time for DIY unless you're filing the EZ form. We lost large amounts of money having the wrong accountants (and attorneys) for our businesses. We would've lost even more doing our own taxes.

If you've got anything complex going on—a business, kids, houses, exemptions, deductions, legal issues like divorce, trust funds, investments, financial windfalls, bankruptcy, or tax baggage—find the right accountant and attorney if you need one. Don't skimp here. There's a reason the wealthiest Americans don't pay taxes: They know the rules and how to use them to their advantage.

Paying experts is worth it.

Be Organized

Vinnie Fisher is an author, accountant, and tax attorney. He's the owner of Fully Accountable, an accounting and office solutions firm for small businesses. Vinnie advises people to make a standing weekly date to log receipts and organize finances and deductions. This way, nothing gets crumpled in the wash or forgotten. Maintain a spreadsheet for deductions and expenses or use Quickbooks. Scan your receipts or keep an organized folder by month.

"I'll do it later. I'll remember."

No, I won't.

Laziness costs money when it comes to taxes. There's a direct mathematical correlation between procrastination and loss. The more I listen to Vinnie, the less I give to Uncle Sam. If I keep organized, I save big. Now, I keep a log sheet in the car where I write mileage and clip receipts, and I follow Vinnie's advice to block off regular time to update my spreadsheets regularly.

Most people know about the standard "teacher deduction" allowed on taxes, but there may be others you never considered, especially if you're freelancing or consulting on the side. Things like travel and home office allowances can add up.

Tax laws changed significantly in 2017 for the 2018 tax year forward, so you'll want to keep receipts and get proper advice.

Consult with your accountant and keep organized. You might just net a large refund.

EPILOGUE
Some Rays of Hope

*"It is not the man who has too little, but the man
who craves more, that is poor."*
—Seneca

I took a deep breath and walked into the store. There were only two other customers—a man in a Rockefeller suit and a lady in a fur coat. And now, there was me.

Tiffany's isn't like other stores in the mall. It's exclusive. There are no visible price tags. If you have to ask, you shouldn't be there to begin with.

Most stores have sales teens glued to their phones. Not Tiffany & Co. It's guarded by a seven-foot-tall giant with a Secret Service earpiece. He stands inside two heavy doors.

Tiffany's? said the voice in my head. *You can't shop at Tiffany's.*

I wasn't planning on shopping. I was planning on drinking coffee while I waited for my phone battery to be swapped. Then I noticed the Tiffany's-deco Christmas tree. It was beautiful. When I heard the voice say I couldn't go in, I had to defeat it.

It wasn't the "can't" that bothered me, it was the tone. *It wasn't saying I don't think you should spend 10 grand on jewelry today* so much as *You don't belong there.*

If I wanted to defeat the voice, I had to march into Tiffany's like any other Vanderbilt with full intent to buy.

I opened the door.

"Hello." I expected Security Giant to be gruff, to be the gatekeeper scanning my wallet, bouncing me out the door. He was friendly.

I can't watch this.... The voice ducked behind the tree. You don't belong here.

I confessed my plan. "I've had some financial disasters, but I'm making a comeback. I'm picking out something nice for myself for when I do."

He smiled. I bet he had a "someday" diamond picked out, too.

The problem with a "someday diamond" is this: *Someday* will always remain *someday* unless I take action. With a little voice constantly reminding me of my station in life, someday is a guaranteed never.

The saleswoman came over right away. "Beautiful ring. Garnet?"

She was complimenting my ring, not Tiffany's. I didn't expect that.

"Yes." I told her the story of the garnet ring. I bought it when I finished my first book. I don't have much jewelry. The little I have is simple and has significance. "These are beautiful," I said, gesturing toward the jewelry behind the glass. "My birthstone—"

"Ah, April," she said. It sounded nice when she said it, not like when it was on notices from Uncle Sam.

She leaned in to speak. She was letting me in on a secret. "They *are* beautiful. They're all elegant and timeless."

Simple. Elegant. Beautiful. Valuable.

Like me. It was the voice again, but this time a different voice, one filled with love. *You are a diamond, too.*

I picked out a ring. It was a rectangle surrounded by two small, roundish triangles on a thin, tapering platinum band. Three stones, just like my garnet ring, except $15,000 more. I looked at it for a moment, shifting funds in my mind while the voice quivered behind the tree. "I'll just make more" didn't yet cover this large a purchase.

But I wasn't really looking for a diamond. I was looking for something else. I wasn't sure what it was when I opened the door, but at that moment, looking at the diamond, talking to Security Giant and Saleswoman, I knew.

It was my value.

I saw it in the way they smiled and treated me with respect, as if I were a real customer and not a "someday" shopper.

And I saw it in myself in the way I believed them and stood a little taller. That's when I knew it wasn't about the ring, the budget, or the number in the bank. "Value" was potential, building myself up and never letting anyone—a person, a job, a curveball situation—cut me down again.

At that moment, I was a billionaire. I told myself this: "You're not Broke Teacher anymore. You are the kind of person who can shop at Tiffany's if she wants, because you can conquer the world."

I put the ring back on the tray. It served its purpose. I thanked the saleswoman and Security Giant. I stopped to admire the Tiffany's tree on the way out the door. The discouraging voice was gone.

Simple. Elegant. Beautiful. Valuable. Like me. That voice remained.

That feeling—that's the feeling I want for every teacher. For every person, really. That feeling of pricelessness, power, and joy.

One day, I gave a talk at a school. I told broke teacher jokes then asked this question: "Where do you find value?" I got the expected answers.

"Coupons." No.

"Sales." Not anymore.

Value comes from knowing I have the power to accomplish anythingin knowing—seeing when I'm out of alignment that I possess and making the change. It's knowing the answer to, "Will this get me to where I want to go?"

It's treating myself well and accepting no less from the world.

I used to confuse value with "cheap" and "frugal."

There's a big difference. Value *creates*. It builds in order to produce big things. Frugal *subtracts* until the balance sheet adds up to zero. The objective isn't zero. , though: It's more. Much more.

It took a long time, but I now see how my "teacher skills" give me the power to reach my goals and dreams. Yours do, too.

Let's all wave goodbye to the broke teacher inside and start moving toward those "someday" goals—whether it's being debt free, saving for retirement, or a cruise with a drink umbrella. Doesn't matter... you'll get there...as long as you leave "broke teacher" behind.

...It is my deepest hope for you that you will.

THANK YOU!

No book or project happens alone. I'd like to thank the usual suspects, and this time a few more. As always, my family, (Mom, Dad, Rusty, Declan, Brittany and Jon, Mary, Brandon, Carter, Dan, Ali, Aidan, Colin, Owen, and Finn, aka "Spike") who listened to my teacher stories much more than they wanted.

A special thanks to Meggan Orenstein, Elly Kennedy, and Sheena Nelson who helped with specific sections of this book.

I'm grateful to Liz LaFrance not only for being a friend, realist, and support, but for sending an impromptu cover design when I was stuck in limbo. It's on this book now. Liz is also the friend in Chapter 5. She and her husband Garrett are the creatives behind *Blocks and Spots*. You can find them online and on YouTube where Garrett puts *This Old House* to shame.

Amanda Maculan came up with the concept that eventually became this cover. She's got one of the biggest hearts in teaching, too.

A big thanks to Alicia Sullivan, my "let's build this" and "get it done" friend who not only *gets* the world of teaching (so I don't get the "shut up about school" look), she's the besta teacher and educational coach in the world. ,You can find her work on *WriteSolutions.com* or at TeachersPayTeachers.

Thank you to Nate Granzow for editing this book even after it took me forever to send the manuscript, and to Brandon Webb for connecting us. Brandon and Nate are both authors you should read. Nate writes fiction, and Brandon is a former Navy Seal and founder and CEO of Hurricane Media. I've given his book *The*

Red Circle to students—nonreaders *who read the whole thing.* Brandon's *Mastering Fear* reinforced the way I now tackle the types of problems in this book. I wish it had been out a decade earlier.

Thank you to Mark Kern who stopped the presses and gave critical thoughts as I was getting ready to push the button. *Broke Teacher* is much better because of him.

Amy Bednarz is the reason *Broke Teacher* exists. Without her it would be little more than a series of Facebook jokes and a small website full of criminally-frugal ideas. She asked me to write it. I'm glad I did.

Thank you to Gwen Duralek, Jennifer Browne, and Beth Isenberg. I used Beth's story in this book. Jennifer is my personal Gabe Kotter. Gwen gave me some of my all-time greatest hits history lessons free of charge. If you're a parent and your kid's still walking around singing "Fleas on Rats," from ten or fifteen years ago, thank Gwen.

I'd also like to thank two teachers on the national stage who dedicate their voices to lifting teachers up--Nick Ferroni spotlights teachers and LGBTQ youth every chance he gets, yet still teaches a full schedule. Angela Maiers' slogan "You Matter," and Choose2Matter organization make a difference to teachers and students worldwide.

Finally, thank you to Kamal Ravikant. He's the friend who taught many of the lesson-stories in this book, and a magnificent author himself. He's the Hemingway to my Tolstoy--he never lets me get away with extra paragraphs or adverbs, which saves everyone a lot of pain. It's because of him I wrote my first book. He helped me "clean the window" and see education in a new way (read his *Love Yourself Like Your Life Depends on It* for that lesson). That changed my teaching and my life, really.

Most of all, thank you to the millions of unnamed teachers who live this life every day. You work three jobs, take on student loan debt, work in low-paying districts or in the toughest assignments, yet still come back every year to inspire. I'm deeply honored you read this book.

If you enjoyed *A Broke Teacher's Guide to Success*, I hope you'll read my first book, *Don't Sniff the Glue: A Teacher's Misadventures in Education Reform.*

I'd be grateful if you left a review on Amazon or Goodreads for either or both, and I'd love to hear from you. You can find me here:

Twitter and Instagram: @runningdmc

Newsletter: broketeacher.com

Email: dawn@broketeacher.com.

ABOUT THE AUTHOR

"You need to write for real," said my friend Kamal.

I promised I would. I kept that promise. That's how I became an author. This is my second book.

These days I live in rural Rhode Island with my family, chickens, and dogs, on what I call my "poser homestead." I call it the Poser Homestead because real preppers are hardcore, and I usually end up at the grocery store after I kill all the food I tried to grow. Still, I'm trying to waste less, live simply, and get a little more off the grid.

I've written about education, clean eating, family life, growing my own food, and luxury frugal living.

I've also co-written a couple of children's books with the amazing cartoonist Sara Steenland, and I've written for or been featured in EdTech Digest, Edutopia, EdSurge, EdWeek, US News & World Report Money, EdTech Review India, ConversationEd, TeachThought, National Public Radio, and Quartz on issues of education technology, financial literacy, frugal foodie and scratch cooking, education reform, and lifestyle.

I've worked in insurance, restaurants, and fitness. I've run the art department at a day camp, supersized fries, and taught martial arts. I fired myself from my own business to become a classroom teacher. I ended up working for an amazing Silicon Valley start-up by accident, asking, "Start-up what?" I've been in tech ever since.

My dream is to get off the grid while still having very fast internet. I don't know if it's possible, but I continue to try.

You can find me on Instagram and Twitter (@runningdmc), on Facebook (facebook.com/broketeacher), or at dawn@broketeacher.com. I'd be honored if you reached out.

RESOURCES

Instead of a formal bibliography, I made a resource list organized by topic. I included several books and articles I didn't directly use in the manuscript, but I found them valuable. I hope you do, too.

On this list you'll find marketing people, psychology experts, coaches, world-class entrepreneurs, venture capitalists, motivators, organizers, farmers, sustainability experts, financial planners, chefs, and Navy SEALs. Some are examples, but a few are "anti-examples." Each has a critical lesson I've applied to my life.

One category of books is intentionally missing: education books. There's a reason for that.

If I stay inside my own small world, I won't learn about the universe. It's only when I escape my corner of the planet that I can grow. That's what I did here. Take this list and read what serves you.

Budgeting and Savings

Gensler, Lauren and Laura Shin. *Money Hacks: Forbes Stories of Superstar Savers.* Amazon: e-book, 2015.

Kiyosaki, Robert, and Sharon Lechter. *Rich Dad, Poor Dad: What the Rich Teach Their Kids about Money that the Poor and Middle Class Do Not.* New York: Warner Business Books, 1997.

Orman, Suze. *Women & Money: Owning the Power to Control Your Destiny*. New York: Spiegel & Grau, 2010

Orman, Suze. *The Money Book for the Young, Fabulous, and Broke*. New York: Spiegel & Grau, 2010

Orman, Suze. *The 9 Steps to Financial Freedom: Practical and Spiritual Steps So You Can Stop Worrying*. New York: Random House, 1997.

Ramsay, Dave. *Total Money Makeover*. Nashville: Nelson Books, 2003.

Robbins, Tony. *Money—Master the Game: 7 Simple Steps to Financial Freedom*. Simon & Schuster, 2014.

Seigel, Cary. *Why Didn't They Teach Me This in School: 99 Personal Money Management Principles to Live By*. CreateSpace, 2013.

Sethi, Ramit. *I Will Teach You to Be Rich*. New York: Workman Publishing, 2009.

Food and Frugal Living

Alexander, William. *The $64 Tomato: How One Man Nearly Lost His Sanity, Spent a Fortune, and Endured an Existential Crisis in the Quest for the Perfect Garden*. Chapel Hill: Algonquin Books) 2007.

Brewer, Annie Jean. *The Shoestring Girl: How I Live on Practically*

Nothing and You Can Too. Createspace, 2012

Freed, Dolly. *Possom Living: How to Live Well Without a Job and With (almost) No Money*. New York: Tin House Books, 1978.

Kingsolver, Barbara. *Animal, Vegetable, Miracle: A Year of Food Life*. New York: Harper Collins, 2007.

Pollan, Michael. *Food Rules*. New York: Penguin, 2009.

Negotiation

Fisher, Roger and William Ury. *Getting to Yes: Negotiating without Giving In*. New York: Penguin Books, 1981.

Galinsky, Adam and Maurice Schweitzer. *Friend & Foe: When to Cooperate, When to Compete, and How to Succeed at Both*. New York: Crown Publishing, 2015.

Freelancing, Work, and the New Economy

Altucher, James. *Choose Yourself*. New York: Lioncrest Publishing, 2013

Altucher, James. *Reinvent Yourself*. New York: Choose Yourself Media, 2016.

Amoruso, Sophia. *#GirlBoss*. New York: Penguin, 2014.

Holiday, Ryan. *Trust Me, I'm Lying: Confessions of a Media*

Manipulator. New York: Penguin Books, 2012.

Shin, Laura. *The Millennial Game Plan: Career and Money Secrets to Succeed in Today's World.* Amazon e-book, 2014.

Inspiration, Self-improvement, and Productivity

Altucher, James and Claudia Azula. *The Power of No: Because One Little Word Can Bring Health, Abundance, and Happiness.* New York: Hay House, 2014.

Azula, Claudia. *Become an Idea Machine: Because Ideas Are the Currency of The 21st Century.* New York: Claudia Azula, 2015.

Davis, Eric. *Raising Men.* New York: St. Martin's Press, 2016.

Ferriss, Timothy. *The Four Hour Chef.* Amazon Publishing, 2012.

Ferriss, Timothy. *The Four Hour Work Week.* New York: Random House, 2009.

Ford, Debbie. *The Best Year of Your Life.* New York: Harper Collins, 2005.

Godin, Seth. *The Icarus Deception.* New York: Penguin Group, 2012.

Godin, Seth. *The Purple Cow.* New York: Penguin Group, 2009.

Grant, Adam. *Give and Take: Why Helping Others Drives Our Success.* New York: Penguin, 2013.

Grant, Adam. *Originals: How Non-Conformists Move the World.* New York: Viking, 2016.

Holiday, Ryan and Stephen Hanselman. *The Daily Stoic: 366 Meditations on Wisdom, Perseverance, and the Art of Living.* (New York: Penguin) 2016.

Kondo, Marie. *The Life-Changing Magic of Tidying Up.* New York: Crown Publishing, 2014.

Latimore, Ed. *The Four Confidences.* http://www.edlatimore.com.
PDF Edition

Ravikant, Kamal. *Live Your Truth* San Francisco: Lioncrest, 2014.

Ravikant, Kamal. *Love Yourself Like Your Life Depends on It.* Lioncrest:
Create Space, 2012. Revised edition: New York: HarperOne,
2020.

Richardson, Cheryl. *The Art of Extreme Self Care: Transform Your Life
One Month at a Time.* New York: Hay House, 2009.

Thoreau, Henry David. *Walden: A Life in the Woods.* 1854. Available in
the Public Domain.

Webb, Brandon, and John David Mann. *Mastering Fear.* New York:
Penguin Group, 2018

Webb, Brandon and John David Mann. *The Power of Thought: Core
Principles to Overcome Adversity and Achieve Success.* New
York: Brandon Webb, 2016.

Fiction

Cervantes, Miguel. *Man of La Mancha*

Ravikant, Kamal. *Rebirth.* New York: Hachette, 2016.

Articles and Sources

All Things Considered. "If You Build Affordable Housing for Teachers,
They Will Come." Directed by Jess Clark. *National Public Radio.*
Dec. 8, 2015. http://www.npr.org/sections
ed/2015/12/08/457994876/if-you-build-affordable-housing-
for-teachers-will-they-come.

Barker, Eric. "How to Negotiate Salary: 5 Secrets Backed by Research."
Barking Up the Wrong Tree. Accessed Dec. 26, 2015. http://
www.bakadesuyo.com/2016/03/how-to-negotiate-salary/.

Ben-Ora, Talia Jane. "An open letter to my CEO" Medium. Feb. 19, 2016.

https://medium.com/@taliajane/an-open-letter-to-my-ceo-fb73df021e7a#.gms0n1rcm.

Census.gov "Median and Average Square Feet of Floor Area in New Single-Family Houses Completed by Location," https://www.census.gov/const/C25Ann/sftotalmedavgsqft.pdf

College Board. "Average Rates of Growth of Published Charges by Decade." *The College Board.* 2016. https://trends.collegeboard.org/content/average-rates-growth-published-charges-decade-0

Currier, Erin and Sheida Elmi. "The State of American Family Finances." The Pew Charitable Trusts. Jan. 7, 2016. http://www.pewtrusts.org/en/research-and-analysis/analysis/2016/01/07/the-state-of-american-family-finances.

Currier, Erin and Joanna Biernacka-Lievestro, Diana Elliott, Sheida Elmi, Clinton Key, Walter Lake, and Sarah Sattelmeyer. "The Precarious State of Family Balance Sheets." *Pew Charitable Trust.* Jan. 2015. http://www.pewtrusts.org/~/media/assets/2015/01/fsm_balance_sheet_report.pdf

Dejardins, Jeff. "A 75-Year History of How Americans Spend Their Money," *Business Insider.* Dec. 20, 2016. http://www.businessinsider.com/how-americans-spend-their-money-2016-12

Dishman, Lydia. "How the Master's Degree Became The New Bachelor's In the Hiring World." *Fast Company.* March 17, 2016. http://www.fastcompany.com/3057941/the-future-of-work/how-the-masters-degree-became-the-new-bachelors-in-the-hiring-world.

Dominos, Susan. "Is Giving the Secret to Getting Ahead?" *The New York Times Magazine.* March 27, 2013. http://www.nytimes.com/2013/03/31/magazine/is-giving-the-secret-to-getting-ahead.html.

El Issa, Erin. "2015 American Household Credit Card Debt Study. Nerdwallet. Accessed Jan. 29, 2016. http://www.nerdwallet.com/blog/credit-card-data/average-credit-card-debt-household/.

Ferriss, Timothy and Naval Ravikant. Podcast: "The Person I Call Most for Startup Advice." Aug.18, 2015. http://fourhourworkweek. com/2015/08/18/the-evolutionary-angel-naval-ravikant/

Gwynn, David. "A Quick History of the Supermarket." Groceteria.com. Accessed Jan. 10, 2016. http://www.groceteria.com/about/a-quick-history-of-the-supermarket/.

HUD.Gov "About Good Neighbor Next Door." *US Department of Housing and Urban Development.* Accessed Feb. 1, 2016. http://portal. hud.gov/hudportal/HUD?src=/program_offices/housing/sfh/ reo/goodn/gnndabot.

Internal Revenue Service. Topic *458: Educator Expense Deduction.* Dec. 30, 2015. https://www.irs.gov/taxtopics/tc458.html.

Isaacson, Betsy. "'Teachers Village' Developers Have Big Dreams for Downtown Newark." *Huffington Post.* Sept. 25, 2013. http:// www.huffingtonpost.com/2013/09/25/teachers-village-newark_n_3991678.html.

Kang, Cecilia. "Building a Digital Divide that Leaves Schoolchildren Behind." *New York Times.* Feb. 2, 2016. http://www.nytimes. com/2016/02/23/technology/fcc-internet-access-school.html.

Knight, Heather. "$20,000 Home Loans for SF Teachers Find Few Takers." *San Francisco Chronicle.* May 27, 2016. http://www. sfchronicle.com/bayarea/article/20-000-home-loans-for-SF-teachers-find-few-takers-7950832.php.

Leff, Lisa. "To Stem Teacher Shortages, School Districts and Cities Think about Becoming Landlords." *US News & World Report.* Jan.2, 2016. http://www.usnews.com/news/us/articles/2016-01-02/ cities-look-at-subsidized-housing-to-stem-teacher-shortages.

Lowry, Annie. "All My Trash Fits in a Single Mason Jar." *New York Magazine.* Dec. 23, 2014. http://nymag.com/daily/ intelligencer/2014/12/all-my-trash-fits-in-a-single-mason-jar. html.

Lowe, Jamie and Brian Ulrich. "The Second Shift: What Teachers are

Doing to Pay Their Bills." *New York Times Magazine*, September 6, 2017. https://www.nytimes.com/interactive/2018/09/06/magazine/teachers-america-second-jobs.html

Madda, Mary Jo. "Arrested Development for Teacher-Led Startups." *EdSurge.* Oct. 22, 2013. https://www.edsurge.com/news/2013-10-22-arrested-development-when-teachers-are-blocked-from-building-edtech-products.

Manni, Tim. "The Salary You Must Own to Buy a Home in 27 Metros." *HSH.com.* Aug. 22, 2016. http://www.hsh.com/finance/mortgage/salary-home-buying-25-cities.html.

Maune Tess. "Education, City Leaders Join Forces on Vision Tax To Benefit Teachers." NewsOn6.com. March 24, 2016. "http://www.newson6.com/story/31560795/education-city-leaders-join-forces-on-vision-tax-to-benefit-teachers.

Mihm, Stephen. "Americans are Living Large As Ever." Bloomberg. June 21, 2017. "https://www.bloomberg.com/view/articles/2017-06-21/americans-are-living-as-large-as-ever"

Mitchell, Travis. "Chart: See 20 Years of Tuition Growth at National Universities." US News & World Report. July 29, 2015. http://www.usnews.com/education/best-colleges/paying-for-college/articles/2015/07/29/chart-see-20-years-of-tuition-growth-at-national-universities.

McCormally, Kevin. "The Most Overlooked Tax Deductions." *Kiplinger.* Jan. 4, 2016. http://www.kiplinger.com/article/taxes/T054-C000-S001-the-most-overlooked-tax-deductions.html.

Mongeau, Lilian. "Is Silicon Valley Driving Teachers Out?" *The Atlantic.* July 21, 2015. http://www.theatlantic.com/education/archive/2015/07/silicon-valley-housing-tough-on-teachers/399071/.

Muy, Ylan. "The Shocking Number of Americans Who Can't Cover a $400 Expense." Washington Post. May 25, 2016. https://www.washingtonpost.com/news/wonk/wp/2016/05/25/the-shocking-number-of-americans-who-cant-cover-a-400-expense/.

My 403 B Coach. "75 Tax Deductions for Teachers." *Mr403B.com*. Oct.16, 2016. http://my403bcoach.com/tax-deductions-for-teachers/.

Nark, Jason. "Is Newark the Next Brooklyn?" *Politico*. March 19, 2015. http://www.politico.com/magazine/story/2015/03/newark-new-jersey-development-what-works-116234.

NEA Member Benefits. "Are You Missing Out on These Educator Tax Benefits?" *NEA*. Dec. 21, 2015. http://www.neamb.com/finance/dont-miss-these-educator-tax-deductions.htm.

Oklahoma Housing Finance Agency. "OHFA 4 Teachers." *OK.gov*. https://www.ok.gov/ohfa/Homebuyers/OHFA_4_Teachers.html.

Picchi, Aimee. "Earning $75,000 and Living Paycheck to Paycheck." *CBS Moneywatch*. April 17, 2015. http://www.cbsnews.com/news/earning-75000-and-living-paycheck-to-paycheck/.

Picchi, Aimee. "The Sorry State of America's Household Finances." *CBS Moneywatch*. January 29, 2015. http://www.cbsnews.com/news/the-sorry-state-of-americas-household-finances/.

Picchi, Aimee. "Why Middle-Class wealth is Withering." *CBS Moneywatch*. Dec. 12, 2014. http://www.cbsnews.com/news/why-middle-class-wealth-is-withering/.

Powell, Eileen Alt. "Lingering Christmas Bills Can Lead to Debt Woes." *ABC News*. March 7, 2016. http://abcnews.go.com/Business/story?id=88539&page=1.

Rao, Krishna. Zillow Rent Index by Tier: Low-end Demand, High-end Supply. *Zillow*. July 27, 2016. http://www.zillow.com/research/zillow-rent-index-tiers-12845/.

Reilly, Katie. "13 Stories of Life on a Teacher's Salary." Time. September 13, 2018. http://time.com/longform/teacher-pay-salary-stories/.

Russell, James. Bloomberg.com October 14, 2013. http://www.bloomberg.com/news/articles/2013-10-14/goldman-richardmeier-boost-149-million-newark-project.

Sethi, Ramit. "The Psychology of Cutting Back on Lattes," *I Will Teach You To Be Rich Blog.* June 8, 2011. http://www. iwillteachyoutoberich.com/blog/save-on-coffee/.

Smith, Ana Sarafin. "Back to School and College Spending to Reach $75.8B" National Retail Federation. July 21, 2016. https://nrf. com/media/press-releases/back-school-and-college-spending-reach-758-billion.

Sparshott, Jeffrey. "Congratulations, Class of 2015. You're the Most Indebted Ever (For Now). *Wall Street Journal.* May 8, 2015. http://blogs.wsj.com/economics/2015/05/08/congratulations-class-of-2015-youre-the-most-indebted-ever-for-now/

Suttle, Rick. "Average Pay for Teacher Recruitment Jobs." *Houston Chronicle.* Accessed January 12, 2016. http://work.chron.com/ average-pay-teacher-recruitment-jobs-19803.html.

"Teacher Discounts for House Prices." *Education World* 2000. http:// www.educationworld.com/a_issues/issues136.shtml

"Teacher Home Loans." Texas State Affordable Housing Corporation. 2016. http://www.tsahc.org/homebuyers-renters/teacher-home-loans

Teachers Village. http://www.teachersvillage.com, accessed Jan. 25, 2016.

Tepper, Taylor. "Americans Are Sinking Further Into Credit Card Debt." *Time.* Dec. 9, 2015. http://time.com/money/4138675/ americans-credit-card-debt-nerdwallet/.

The Hechinger Report. "Heaviest Debt Burdens Fall on 3 Types of Students." *US News & World Report.* June 8, 2015. http://www. usnews.com/news/articles/2015/06/08/heaviest-college-debt-burdens-fall-on-3-types-of-students.

Time, Forest. "The Average Beginning Teacher Salaries." *Houston Chronicle.* Accessed Jan. 12, 2016. http://work.chron.com/ average-beginning-teacher-salaries-1364.html.

Tucker, Jill. "To Attract Teachers, Schools Get into the Housing Business." San Francisco Chronicle. October 26, 2015. http://www.sfchronicle.com/bayarea/article/To-attract-teachers-school-districts-get-into-6591925.php.

Udland, Myles. "Housing Is So Outrageously Expensive in San Francisco The City Can't Hire Enough Teachers." *Business Insider.* Aug. 4, 2015. http://www.businessinsider.com/san-francisco-teachers-cant-afford-to-live-2015-8.

US Inflation Calculator. "Current US Inflation Rates, 2006–2016." *Coin News Media Group, LLC.* Accessed Jan. 20, 2016. http://www.usinflationcalculator.com/inflation/current-inflation-rates/.

Weagley, Robert. "One Big Difference Between Chinese and American Households: Debt." *Forbes.* June 24, 2010. http://www.forbes.com/sites/moneybuilder/2010/06/24/one-big-difference-between-chinese-and-american-households-debt/#60e145382a67.

Weise, Karen. "Housing's 30-Percent-of-Income Rule Is Nearly Useless." Bloomberg. July 17, 2014. http://www.bloomberg.com/bw/articles/2014-07-17/housings-30-percent-of-income-rule-is-near-useless.

Wendler, Emily. "Teacher of the Year in Oklahoma Moves to Texas for the Money." NPR. July 2, 2017. http://www.npr.org/sections/ed/2017/07/02/531911536/teacher-of-the-year-in-oklahoma-moves-to-texas-for-the-money

Williams, Geoff. "Are You A Supermarket Snob?" US News & World Report. May 8, 2015. http://money.usnews.com/money/personal-finance/articles/2015/05/08/are-you-a-supermarket-snob.

Winters, Michael. "Graph of the Week" Where Are Teachers Really Paid Most?" *EdSurge*. Feb. 4, 2015. https://www.edsurge.com/news/2015-02-04-graph-of-the-week-where-are-teachers-really-paid-most.

Wong, Kristin. "How to Protect Your Credit When You Marry Into Debt." *Lifechacker*. May 15, 2014. http://twocents.lifehacker.com/how-to-protect-your-credit-when-you-marry-into-debt-1576458795.

Zimmer, Amy. "Pre-K Teachers Are on Food Stamps After 10 Years Without a Raise." *DNA Info*. Dec. 29, 2015. http://www.dnainfo.com/new-york/20151229/bushwick/pre-k-teachers-are-on-food-stamps-after-10-years-without-raise.

Made in the
USA
Middletown, DE